# The DECEITFULNESS of RELIGION

## IT MATTERS WHAT YOU BELIEVE

*Augustin D. Etienne*

The Reading Glass
BOOKS

The DECEITFULNESS of RELIGION:
**It Matters What You Believe**
Copyright © 2022 by Augustin D. Etienne

ISBN:   (Paperback)      978-1959151081
        (eBook)          978-1959151098

The Reading Glass
BOOKS

# CONTENTS

# ACKNOWLEGEMENTS

But thanks be to God which giveth us the
victory through our Lord Jesus Christ
- *I Corinthians 15:57*

Special thanks go to God who has, not only commissioned this work, but has also enabled the writing and completion of the work. Without His aid this work would not be possible. It was with great difficulty that the last few chapters of this book came together and were it not for the grace of God, they might have been impossible. To say, "I can do all things through Christ who strengthens me" is not only a scripture verse, but became a reality as I struggled with writing. Not that the information was not readily available but spiritual oppression was very obvious.

Thanks go to my family for their understanding during the long hours that it took to write. This sometimes required late nights when everyone else was asleep. Moving around at those late hours sometimes created disturbances that affected sound sleep. Thanks to my wife Gloria, and daughter Hermione who is still at home for their patience and understanding.

Special thanks to Mrs. Oswalla Rodney for her painstaking effort in editing the manuscript. Identifying the numerous typographical and structural errors was testimony of the time and diligence applied in undertaking the task. Thanks, too, to Alfea Henry and Mrs. Najhdla Dilsuk for their contributions in editing the work.

Thanks again to God for affording me the privilege of undertaking such a task for His honor and glory. It is not because of any special ability that I was challenged but because, as He said, "He has chosen the foolish things of the world to confound the wise."

# FORWARD

# DECEITFULNESS OF RELIGION

**It matters what you believe**

This treatise is not meant to explore the origins and longevity of early religions, neither is it meant to delineate present day religions but rather to expose the inadequacies of all which do not offer the eternal hope which God determined and to offer a solution to the dilemma of worshipers. Limited reference to early and ancient religions is made because I want to get quickly to the problem of the many departures from truth and to establish the truth in such a way that one would desire to accept it.

It was Christ who said: "Ye worship, ye know not what." Many are ardent worshipers but are not cognizant that they merely worship tradition and not a living Savior. For some, their forms and practices are deeply steeped in ancestral transmissions and cultural practices rather than in an active faith which holds out hope. Others, on the other hand, have sought to disassociate themselves with seemingly irrational tradition and have flung themselves to the other extreme of either creating a religion with personal morality which suits their fancies or disavow the existence of any. Still others are not organized to the extent of having established buildings or recognized affiliates, but by their practices are religions.

This is meant to redirect one's thinking to God who has consistently declared Himself historically and through His written Word; to a God who has been personally involved in the lives of humankind in supernatural, yet experiential ways which leave incontrovertible evidence of His existence. Even now, through the accuracy of prophetic writings, He shows himself to be the Omniscient One who declares "the end from the beginning". The fulfillment of prophecy should do nothing but propel one into the arms of a loving and waiting God. Instances of judgments should not serve to deter one from God, but should guide one away from the pitfalls to which many have been subjected. Warnings of impending danger are not without impressive spiritual and physical hope which should goad one in the desired direction of a God who seeks to have fellowship, not with robots, but with his creatures, who, through their own volition, opt to serve Him.

# CHAPTER ONE

# WHAT IS RELIGION

Religion seems to be one of the most common, yet the most controversial subjects of man's experiences. There is not a society - ancient, primitive or contemporary - which does not have a form of religion, regardless of how simple or complex its form. Religion permeates the lifestyle of all its adherents; even of those who unwittingly practice a form of religion which is non-conforming or non-traditional. It is expansive in scope, and despite modern attempts to define and/or to redefine it, religion embraces a wide variety of beliefs which today may be outside the limits of its definition.

One of the most fundamental aspects of religion is belief in a supreme being. The operation characteristic of this concept is that there is belief or faith. One believes in a Supreme Being or 'force' responsible for the origin, balance and sustenance of one's existence upon earth. On the other hand there are those who do not accept or accede to a supreme but subscribe to a set of beliefs contrary to and counterpoint formal religion in such a way that it renders such a body of tenets a religion without the expressed intention of its proponents.

One recognizes that not all beliefs are religions. One's belief in science may be recognition of prescribed laws that govern the movement of earth and factors which regulate its daily running. Such recognition comes as a result of much observation and study and is universally understood because these are constant and recognizable. They comply with the acknowledged scientific principles which are practical and repeatable. These do not necessarily delve into matters of the heart neither are they colored with matters of mere faith in a deity.

Having excluded true scientific exercises from the realm of faith, one must also recognize that science and many other disciplines are brought under the umbrella of religion when they are packaged as mere beliefs and not observable scientific processes. This may also be so when one treats these disciplines as matters of absolutes and veneration. Only God is to be worshipped. When one replaces the one worshipped with any object or discipline, that substitute becomes one's "supreme" and thus a religion. These are idols in immaterial forms.

Religion, nonetheless, encompasses numerous forms and descriptions; from the most basic and primitive to the modern and elaborate. Religion, in early times, was closely related to the culture of a society and oftentimes formed the basis of their laws and social practices. A clear example of this is the development of the Jewish religion – Judaism. As they were liberated from Egypt and were in the process of establishing themselves as a unique entity, their God, the God of the universe, stamped His presence and authority on their lives in the laws that He commanded that they keep. Their moral laws – the Ten Commandments - begin with God and continue through the fourth commandment. Their civil laws reflected the disposition of their God to every aspect of their social lives. Punishments for violation of each of their laws were prescribed so that justice would be exercised in all their activities.

A close look at other cultures or civilizations reflects similar trends. Each of the nations around had their particular god with their accompanying forms of worship. As Israel was established in their land the most vociferous admonition to them was not to intermingle with their idolatrous neighbors lest they learnt their ways and angered their God. Other nations, too, had apprehensions regarding offending their god. Oftentimes, weather conditions were attributed to particular dispositions of their god. Adverse weather conditions would signify the displeasure of their deity and would often require particular sacrifices to appease him.

Archeological discoveries in the nineteenth and twentieth centuries have disclosed ancient writings which reveal the close affinity of religion with the social fabric of some of the earliest societies of the post flood era. Most of these people lived in the area known as the Near East which extended from the great rivers of Mesopotamia (present day Iran and Iraq) through Egypt in the south. While each people grouping might have had their own writings, two groups, through theirs, stand out. These were namely Mesopotamia (often referred to as the Semites) and Egypt. The Jews, with their unique form of religion different from those around them, occupied the middle ground between those civilizations. What is most astounding is the similarities in their records of the origins and development of human kind.

Bill T. Arnold, in his study entitled *Encountering the Book of Genesis* highlights the records of these ethnic groups. He reports on some of those archeological findings of that period. He writes: "We may presume that all of the peoples surrounding Israel had their own traditions, myths, and legends to explain how the world came into existence. But only the great riverine cultures of Mesopotamia and

Egypt have preserved details of those traditions. These great early civilizations first used writings in a significant way to preserve the theological speculations of humankind. This literature was lost when the first great empires disappeared and lay buried beneath the sands of time for thousands of years. But in the nineteenth and twentieth centuries, archeologists have discovered, deciphered, and translated Egyptian and Mesopotamian accounts of creation and the flood. This relatively recent development has obviously led to a greater understanding of Israel's view of God, the world, and humankind."[1]

Another outstanding phenomenon is the close relationship between the peoples and their deity. It would seem that the histories of these civilizations were each charted by divine intervention into the history of their respective civilizations. The historical records of the Jews are what we find in the Holy Bible. Even the Arabs, though they have a different slant on the same events recorded in the Bible, lay claim to the benefits of the relationship between God and Abraham. Thus we see that religion has played an integral part in the histories of the peoples of this planet.

The author of _The World's Religions_, in its first chapter written by Edward G. Newing writes: "It could be said that a PLS (Pre-literary society) does not have a religion. It is itself a religion, or rather a religious community. Practically every activity, both individual and communal, within the PLS has religious significance. Of course those who belong to a PLS are not conscious of this. That is simply the way they live. This permeation of life with the sacred is a fundamental characteristic of the PLS and cannot be overemphasized, since we who divide life into sacred and secular, with the emphasis on the latter, by this very fact tend to distort what we see in other societies which are different in quality as well as in quantity from our own."[2]

Another author whose reference I failed to secure says, "Religion is a copout for true faith in God. It provides a supposedly spiritual crutch for one's replacement of faith acts required by God."

## But how do we define "Religion"?

We look at some of the formal definitions of "religion" to take in its scope and prevalence in society. These reveal a myriad of areas affected by religion. The definitions we will consider here are from Wikipedia on the World Wide Web. This one states:

A **religion** is a set of beliefs concerning the cause, nature, and purpose of the universe, especially when considered as the creation of a supernatural agency or agencies, usually involving devotional and ritual observances, and often containing a moral code governing the conduct of human affairs.[3]

Aspects of religion include narrative, symbolism, beliefs, and practices that are supposed to give meaning to the practitioner's experiences of life. Whether the meaning centers on a deity or deities, or an ultimate truth, religion is commonly identified by the practitioner's prayer, ritual, meditation, music and art, among other things, and is often interwoven with society and politics. It may focus on specific supernatural, metaphysical, and moral claims about reality (the cosmos and human nature) which may yield a set of religious laws, ethics, and a particular lifestyle. Religion also encompasses ancestral or cultural traditions, writings, history, and mythology, as well as personal faith and religious experience.[4]

One readily notices the many aspects of religion as highlighted in the quotation above. Each of these lends itself to the development of angles and variations in religion. These form a network of divergent roads which should lead to somewhere; but where? They also raise the questions of "Does it really matter what one believes?" or "Does it matter where these roads lead? These are questions that we will attempt to answer, for all roads do not lead to the same destination. Despite the level of passion with which one may approach the topic, the Bible reduces these many roads to just two: the broad road and the narrow road, the right way and the wrong way. All of the ramifications are relative to God.

The definition of "Religion" is further developed as:... the personal practices related to communal faith and to group rituals and communication stemming from shared conviction. "Religion" is sometimes used interchangeably with "faith" or "belief system," but it is more socially defined than personal convictions, and it entails specific behaviors, respectively.

The development of religion has taken many forms in various cultures. It considers psychological and social roots, along with origins and historical development.

Religion is often described as a communal system for the coherence of belief focusing on a system of thought, unseen being, person, or object, that is considered to be supernatural, sacred, divine, or of the highest truth. Moral codes, practices, values, institutions, tradition, rituals, and scriptures are often traditionally associated with the core belief, and these may have some overlap with concepts in secular philosophy. Religion is also often described as a "way of life" or a life stance.[5]

One of the first aspects of religion requiring careful consideration is the matter of a "supernatural agency or agencies". This is a euphemism with reference to God. Various religions may have different names for their 'supreme being' which do not necessarily have reference to the one Christians call God but is none-the-less their ultimate being. This also recognizes that, for some, there are multiple "agencies" who serve the same purpose. Some of these have a division of "labor" where different deities oversee separate aspects of the wide spectrum of responsibilities assigned to their supreme.

**Here is a consideration of deity:**

A **deity** is a postulated preternatural or supernatural immortal being, who may be thought of as holy, divine, or sacred, held in high regard, and respected by believers, often called in some religions as a **god**.

Deities are depicted in a variety of forms, but are frequently expressed as having human or animal form. Some faiths and traditions consider it blasphemous to imagine or depict the deity as having any concrete form. They are usually immortal, and are commonly assumed to have personalities and to possess consciousness, intellects, desires, and emotions similar to those of humans. Such natural phenomena as lightning, floods, storms, other 'acts of God', and miracles are attributed to them, and they may be thought to be the authorities or controllers of various aspects of human life (such as birth or the afterlife). Some deities are asserted to be the directors of time and fate itself, to be the givers of human law and morality, to be the ultimate judges of human worth and behavior, and to be the designers and creators of the earth or the universe.[6] Some deities are thought to be invisible or inaccessible to humans, dwelling mainly in other worldly, remote or secluded and holy places, such as Heaven, Hell, the sky, the under-world, under the sea, in the high mountains or deep forests, or in a supernatural plane or celestial sphere. Typically, they rarely reveal or manifest themselves to humans, and make themselves known mainly through their effects. Monotheistic deities are often thought of as being omnipresent, though invisible.

Often people feel an obligation to their deity, although some view their deity as something that serves them.[7]

These religions follow a prescribed list of observances which their adherents practise.

**Body of truth:**

**Scripture** is that portion of literature deemed authoritative for establishing instructions *within* any of a number of specific religious traditions, especially the Abrahamic religions. Such bodies of writings are also sometimes known as the canon of scripture. They are often associated with the belief that they were either given directly, or otherwise inspired, by God, or associated with other kinds of direct access to absolute truth. As such, the term *scripture* is more specific than *religious text*, which scholars apply even to mythological and ritual texts from ancient religions, where records of their authority (or heresy) have not survived.

Investigations by scholars of comparative religion determine the different reasoning that lies behind why various traditions determine some writings to be scripture and others not.

This can be illustrated by the documentation of the Egyptian cult of Aten, which lasted less than a generation (ca 1350–1335 BC), having been suppressed as heresy. The Nicene Creed is an early Christian description of their beliefs. However, although this is clearly a religious text and is still highly valued by Christians today, it is not considered scripture because it is not among the sacred writings of either the Old or New Testaments. Scriptures are religious texts, the truth of which is received by believers in some traditions based only faith or belief, in that faith is belief in the trustworthiness of a written/spoken idea that has not been proven. However, in the Abrahamic traditions especially, but also in others, the scriptures include documentation of events, and reasoned arguments, so the concept of faith is understood to be based on objective and verifiable facts, not merely "blind trust".[8]

While we will leave this matter for later discussion, I must point out that Scripture, the Bible, is well recognized as factual and reliable. In the previous paragraph it is referred to as 'reasoned arguments', 'objective and verifiable facts, not merely blind trust'. These are very accurate descriptions of the book we know to be the Word of God. One observes very clearly and readily that it is uncompromising, unflattering, and unbiased. Of course one can use this same book to make outlandish claims but because of the divine authorship of the book we know that contrary claims are scurrilous.

## Codes of conduct:

Not all embrace a code of conduct which governs their everyday living, but all develop lifestyles that are affected to a greater or lesser degree by their religion. Some may have particular rules and regulations yet have no assured future but seem to leave the end result to fate. Others hold strongly to beliefs that their conduct here significantly affects their afterlife or next life. As a result their codes of conduct or morality are intricately intertwined into the fabric of their culture.

Codified morality is generally distinguished from custom, another way for a community to define appropriate activity, by the former's derivation from natural or universal principles. In certain religious communities, the Divine is said to provide these principles through revelation, sometimes in great detail. Such codes may be called laws, as in the Law of Moses, or community morality may be defined through commentary on the texts of revelation, as in Islamic law. Such codes are distinguished from legal or judicial right, including civil rights, which are based on the accumulated traditions, decrees and legislation of a political authority, though these latter often invoke the authority of the moral law.

Morality can also be seen as the collection of beliefs as to what constitutes a good life. Since throughout most of human history, religions have provided both visions and regulations for an ideal life, morality is often confused with religious precepts. In secular communities, lifestyle choices, which represent an individual's conception of the good life, are often discussed in terms of morality." Individuals sometimes feel that making an appropriate lifestyle choice invokes a true morality, and that accepted codes of conduct within their chosen community are fundamentally moral, even when such codes deviate from more general social principles.

Moral codes are often complex definitions of moral and immoral that are based upon well-defined value systems. Although some people might think that a moral code is simple, rarely is there anything simple about one's values, ethics, etc. or, for that matter, the judgment of those of others. The difficulty lies in the fact that morals are often part of a religion and more often than not about culture codes. Sometimes, moral codes give way to legal codes, which couple penalties or corrective actions with particular practices. Note that while many legal codes are merely built on a foundation of religious and/or cultural moral codes, often they are one and the same.[9]

## Lifestyles and Religion:

One's behavior pattern is generally referred to as his lifestyle. In more modern times such lifestyles have been redefined and reclassified as life stances. This development came in an effort to so define one's way of living as to remove the stigma of humanist lifestyles as opposed to religious lifestyles. The uniformity of definition removed the distinctions among the wide variety of lifestyles that were not based in a formal religion.

## Wikipedia has this to say of life stance:

*Life stance* is a neologism apparently coined in the mid 1970s by humanists interested in educational matters, and developed originally in that context by Harry Stopes-Roe of the Rationalist Press Association and British Humanist Association. It was originally used in the context of debates over the controversial content of the City of Birmingham's *Agreed Syllabus for Religious Education*, 1975. That document referred to "non-religious stances for living". According to Barnes:

"It was the first syllabus to abandon the aim of Christian nurture and to embrace a multi-faith, phenomenological model of religious education; and it was also the first syllabus to require a *systematic* study of non-religious 'stances for living', such as Humanism, and for such study to begin in the primary school".[10]

One of the main proponents of a change in term or the recognition of the new term which would encompass all lifestyles is "Harry Stopes-Roe of the Rationalist Press Association and British Humanist Association.[11]

## According to Stopes-Roe:

"Life stance" is an expression that has been current in Britain for more than ten years and is now gaining acceptance worldwide, to describe what is good in both Humanism and religion - without being encumbered by what is bad in religion.[12]

Different life stances differ in what they hold as intrinsic values and purposes in life.

For instance, the purpose in Humanism is, in the broadest sense, personality, determined by humans, completely without supernatural influence. For Judaism, on the other hand, it is to serve God and to prepare for the world to come.

What is held as intrinsic value and purpose may differ substantially between individuals regarding themselves as belonging to the same life stance."[13]

Religion, none-the-less, played a major role in the manner of life of the individual. Its mores and norms charted the way a person behaved socially, the way one conducted business, one's values of right and wrong and to some extent dress codes. There were religions recognized by their dress wear. Even today, certain religions are identifiable by their dress styles and literature that they hold out. Religion does continue to affect the lifestyle of individuals within a community.

ENCYCLOPEDIA BRITANICA NOTES+

## Politics and religion:

Strange as it may seem, politics was an integral part of religion. A society is made up of individuals but these individuals adhere to each other because of the common codes that they follow. This was the basis for society and the thread which sustained it down through the years and generations. Established principles and laws were recognized, adhered to and passed on because these are the glue which holds people together.

Again we consider the societies of the Middle East and that of Israel in its existence before Christ to confirm our statement. Wars were very common then and countries ascribed their victories to their God. The Bible is replete, not only with the account of God fighting for His chosen people, the Jews, but also with the trends of the nations around as they engaged in battle. Religious symbols or relics were carried to battle and festivities to their gods were conducted if victorious. Israel, when attacked by the Assyrians were chided that their God was no better than the gods of the nations which the Assyrians had conquered. The God of the Jews was ridiculed and thought to be no better than the idols of the nations around (II Kings 19:33 – 35). Thus He would not be able to deliver them from their hands. Of course the Assyrians found out differently.

Their politics was governed by the type of religion that they practised. Again we use Israel as our example. Israel had a theocracy while most of the nations had monarchies. Israel was ruled by God. In time they turned their backs on God and desired a monarchical style of government (I Samuel 8:1 – 9). Of course that came with their desire to be like their neighbors. Not only did they change their style of government, they also changed their God. They became as idolatrous as the nations around and were consequently thrust out of the land which their God had given them in covenant. Even today, the struggle continues over the land which was their patrimony.

Today, the politics has changed to the extent that it is not the type of national cohesion, but a disjointed and almost dysfunctional entity. There has been a cry for the separation of church and state where these are mutually exclusive. The role and function of one should not affect that of the other. A close look though, will reveal that the desire is for Christianity not to have any say in their lifestyles thus allowing them to live as degenerate a lifestyle as they choose. Other religions that reject God, on the other hand, are allowed their freedoms and even allowed to impose their value structure on societies that favor God. This unveils the hypocrisy of a separation of church and state. Individualism is the norm of the day. As the Bible aptly puts it, "Each man did what was right in his own eyes."

In a very strict sense what has been accomplished is that the religious freedom of Christians is severely challenged to the extent that, if allowed, their constitutional right to freedom of religion will be taken away. Along with this, secularism is being imposed on those who would prefer to recognize a God who rules.

These affronts are being sustained with litigations which hopefully will financially leave the Christians unable to defend their positions legally and by default succumb to the whims and fancies of liberals. These challenges are exemplified in the areas of abortion, the use of religious symbols and relics, the use of words referring to God in public places and sometimes on private property if these are deemed to be in public view. Each challenge becomes a legal issue where the challengers, realizing that they may be better financed and sometime more disposed to pursuing the matter legally; litigate relentlessly until their issue is given legal backing.

Another attempt to "de Christianize" Christian societies is the redefinition of religion. Religion is no longer the politically correct way to refer to one's relationship with the higher powers but it is more appropriate to refer to one's "spirituality". Of course the term is vague and can include any and everything from worshipping one's self to worshipping Satan. The one thing that must not be done is to recognize God as God.

**Here is how Wikipedia states it:**

"Members of an organized religion may not see any significant difference between religion and spirituality. Or they may see a distinction between the mundane, earthly aspects of their religion and its spiritual dimension.

Some individuals draw a strong distinction between religion and spirituality. They may see spirituality as a belief in ideas of religious significance (such as God, the Soul, or Heaven), but not feel bound to the bureaucratic structure and creeds of a particular organized religion. They choose the term *spirituality* rather than religion to describe their form of belief, perhaps reflecting a disillusionment with organized religion (see Major religious groups), and a movement towards a more "modern" — more tolerant, and more intuitive — form of religion. These individuals may reject organized religion because of historical acts by religious organizations, such as Christian Crusades and Islamic Jihad, the marginalisation and persecution of various minorities or the Spanish Inquisition. The basic precept of the ancient spiritual tradition of India, the Vedas, is the *inner reality* of existence, which is essentially a spiritual approach to being."[14]

Religion, then, encompasses a wide sector, if not all of human life. Whether one subscribes to a prescribed form of religion or not, one is affected by the tentacles of religion in one form or another. What becomes crucial is whether there is justification for any particular religion and its tenets or whether all should be discarded or rather treated as unacceptable ancestral customs in this day of 'enlightenment'.

Norman L. Geisler treats the subject extensively in his book *Christian Apologetics*. He presents various world viewpoints and presentations by their major proponents analyzing them logically and exposing their strengths and weaknesses. One thing that is most apparent is that well expressed sentiments do not make for truth. Truth can stand whatever tests it is subjected to.

Several quotations from Geisler should serve to put religion in a perspective from which we can work. In considering Religion as an "Experience" Geisler quotes

Frederich Schleiermacher as saying "Man reject religion as a general idea arbitrarily conceived, but to do so is to look only at the shell and reject the kernel". In view of this, Schleiermacher exhorts his contemporaries to 'turn from everything usually reckoned religion, and fix your regard on the inward emotions and dispositions...'."[15] Geisler continues to quote Schleiermacher who says that "Dogma is only the echo of religion; true religion is an immediate feeling of the Infinite and Eternal."[16] "True religion is related to doctrine the way the original sound is related to an echo. Religion is based in experience and creeds are only expressions of that experience. One is the feeling and the other a form; religious experience is the "stuff" and religious language and ritual the structure of religion. The experience of God is the primary reality and religious thought is but a later reflection on that reality."[17]

Geisler himself states, "Another contrast is helpful in understanding Schleiermacher's concept of religious experience. Ethics is a way of *living*, science is a way of *thinking*, but religion is a way of *feeling*. It is not just any way of feeling but it is the feeling of being utterly dependent on the All. Again ethics is a way of *acting*, science is a way of *knowing*, whereas religion is a way of *being or sensing* one's dependence." [18]

One cannot get away from the fact that he is a religious being. To this Geisler says, "Every man has an inborn capacity for religion which infallibly develops unless it is crushed by culture."[19] Many today deny that there is that feeling but God Himself has declared in His word:

> *For the wrath of God is revealed from heaven against all ungodliness and unrighteousness of men, who hold the truth in unrighteousness; because that which may be known of God is manifest in them; for God hath showed it unto them. For the invisible things of him*

*from the creation of the world are clearly seen, being understood by the things that are made, even his eternal power and Godhead; so that they are without excuse: (Romans 1:18–20)*

It is most fitting to end our definition in the words of Geisler, "A true religion is one that cures human pride and sin."[20]

# CHAPTER TWO

# MISCONCEPTIONS IN AND CONCERNING RELIGION

Religion, by its prevalence, presents itself as something necessary for the existence and future of mankind. One realizes that from antiquity religion has played an integral role in the life of man in all societies in a way that renders it the common thread of all humanity. Regardless of the one worshipped, the manner of such worship, the rituals involved in such worship, the tenets of the religion, the intensity of their worship, one realizes the use of religion in the life of a people. In some cases it would seem that the very existence of a society was to please their supreme. Such religion would find expression in the architecture, literature, and culture of a society regardless of how archaic or modern, simple or developed.

Giving due recognition to the record of world history found in the Bible one cannot but be baffled at the rapidity of the degeneration of man in the realm of religion when one considers the age of Noah and his sons against the rapid development of idolatry in the East following the flood. From the Biblical records we realize that Noah lived for three hundred and fifty years following the flood (Gen. 9:28). His son Shem lived for five hundred years after the flood (Gen. 11:11). Considering the need for the rapid repopulation of the earth we realize that long life was a necessity immediately following the flood. While the Bible does not give us the exact length of time for Ham and Japheth, considering the number of children each produced a comparative analysis with their brother Shem would suggest that they, too, lived for a long time after the flood.

The rationale behind the longevity of the life of these individuals is that these had firsthand experience with the God of the earth. They were the bridge between the generations which existed before the flood and themselves who were now repopulating the earth. They were living testimony of the flood and the lifestyles which warranted its implementation. They were well acquainted with the God who had just destroyed the earth with a universal flood and must have communicated their experiences to their children, grandchildren and great grandchildren since verbal communication was the main way of preserving history for posterity. That firsthand information spanned many generations, and it was available to all who cared to know. These men must have perpetuated the form of sacrifice that Noah offered upon disembarking the Ark. That God was knowable.

One argument which may work in favour of those early inhabitants of the earth is the fact that they had to disperse. They were required to spread over the earth and occupy the lands which lay before them.

Even then man, in rebellion, refused to scatter and chose instead to build one single community with adequate accommodation for the rapidly growing population. The concept of a skyscraper was initiated hoping to provide protection against the eventuality of another flood. Thus we had the Tower of Babel. It took the intervention of God with a confusion of tongues to forestall their plans and to force the dispersion of man according to language groupings. Possibly, these phenomena contributed to the distortion of information available for onward transmission to other generations. Yet one can also reasonably conclude that whatever previous information man had was readily available in each new language. Knowledge did not dissipate with the advent of new languages. Each new language was spoken as though it were one's own native language. Therefore, the historical data passed on should have been consistent with history.

By the time we hear of Abraham, idolatry was commonplace. God had to call him out of an idolatrous civilization. Abraham lived at a time when Noah and his sons were still alive and so might have been exposed to the knowledge expounded by them. (See time charts in this author's previous publication *God at Work* ISBN 975 1 4363 7429 3). One can legitimately lay charge of the multiplicity and confusion of religion at the steps of the Devil. He is the author of confusion and the father of all lies (Jn. 8:44 cf. I Cor. 14:33; II Cor. 11:13 – 15).

The Bible gives us the origin of idolatry within the human race. Romans 1:18 – 23 tell us:

> *For the wrath of God is revealed from heaven against all ungodliness and unrighteousness of men, who hold the truth in unrighteousness; because that which may be known of God is manifest in them; for God hath showed it unto them.*
>
> *For the invisible things of him from the creation of the world are clearly seen, being understood by the things that are made, even his eternal power and Godhead; so that they are without excuse: because that, when they knew God, they glorified him not as*

*God, neither were thankful; but became vain in their imaginations, and their foolish heart was darkened.*

*Professing themselves to be wise, they became fools, and changed the glory of the uncorruptible God into an image made like to corruptible man, and to birds, and four-footed beasts, and creeping things.*

These Scripture verses tell us that God is knowable and God was known; that the decision to worship objects was a deliberate choice; that the knowledge of God exists in the heart and that such knowledge is placed there by God, Himself. This indictment is made by a God who existed and still exists; a God who has full knowledge of all that has transpired; a God who is omniscient. God declares that man is without excuse. Even now the desire to worship is still evident in man, only that he would rather worship something other than God. The desire to form a deity is bred from an inbuilt capacity in man to worship.

With the change of their God came the desire to create alternatives. With the alterations came all ill-conceived notions of reality. Their self-professed wisdom leads them further and further away from the reality that only God is supreme. Thus the Bible says that professing themselves to be wise they became fools. Their alternatives are dumb ideas which seem plausible to them.

Man expresses his inability to think right in all the bad choices he has made. Within the realm of religion, man has conceived that the antiquity of their religion redounds to authenticity so that the older the religion the more assured they are that they are doing the right thing. Today we find that there is a craze for ancient and Middle Eastern religions with the accompanying argument that these were existent before Christianity. Age does not determine truthfulness.

Another criterion for "authentic religion" is the intensity with which its adherents worship. There are those who pray frequently and regularly many times a day in the hope that their zeal will amount to something. There are others who inflict bodily harm to themselves in their quest to connect with their god. Others offer infants as sacrifices in their desire to please their god. All sorts of séances, ritualistic killings and dances are performed in order to make connection with their god. Throwing babies into the fire or river is practised in order to connect with their deity, yet none of these bring peace or lasting hope.

Modern day man postulates that there are many ways to reach God. There is no one religion with a corner on the truth regarding God. Further, each man can forge his own way towards God and will eventually reach Him.

Even within "Christian" circles there are misconceptions of religion. One would have thought that to call one's self 'Christian' would automatically put one into a right relationship with God. It is not so. There are imitations so closely resembling the real thing that Jesus, in speaking to His disciples, informed them that those 'tares' growing among the wheat should be left till the end times. The Father will send His reapers to separate one from the other. That may be so among individuals but there are groupings that show signs and hold on to doctrines that are definitely not authentic regardless of how close to the genuine they may get. These are marked by specific traits that expose their deceitful intentions. Some of these marks we will consider in a subsequent chapter.

**Christian misconceptions:**

In the New Testament of the Bible we experience many misconceptions that we would like to explore here. One of them is the false notion of how much we know intuitively.

One thing we do know is that without the instructions of Christ our knowledge is limited and faulty. In the life of Jesus Christ, His earthly experiences revealed considerable misconceptions. Many thought they knew who or what the Christ would be when He would make His appearance on the earth. The following is one example of the ignorance of Christ's contemporaries and indeed that of many today.

> *Then said some of them of Jerusalem, Is not this he, whom they seek to kill? But, lo, he speaketh boldly, and they say nothing unto him. Do the rulers know indeed that this is the very Christ? Howbeit we know this man whence he is: but when Christ cometh, no man knoweth whence he is.*
>
> *Then cried Jesus in the temple as he taught, saying, Ye both know me, and ye know whence I am: and I am not come of myself, but he that sent me is true, whom ye know not. But I know him: for I am from him, and he hath sent me* (John 7:25 – 29).

Jesus had declared Himself to the people by His words and by the miracles that He did. They well understood the miracles but because of their preconceived ideas of who Christ would be and where He would come from it was hard for them to accept that He was the one, standing among them. Their questions and statements exposed their level of ignorance. On the other hand, their questions revealed a type of thinking which seemed to suggest that they had knowledge which should be kept secret so that the people would not move in His direction.

The first question in the passage quoted above shows a quizzical disposition where confusion seems to prevail. Here is Jesus - One wanted for the purpose of silencing Him in death - teaching among them in their synagogues, yet no one attempts to take Him. It is puzzling because there seems to be a sense of awe which far outweighs the feelings of fear which they possessed. They would love to rid the public of a 'nuisance' which, to them, is not profitable for their 'beloved countrymen'; but for some reason they cannot approach Him with any measure of indignation borne out of moral rectitude which would serve the common good. There seems to be some apprehension that they might do the populace and indeed themselves an irreparable injustice which would leave them the poorer.

Yet their reputation and the status quo were being jeopardized to the extent that if things were allowed to continue they would lose their prominence as leaders of the people. Their expressed fear that the Romans would step in and remove them was the least of their fears. Yet this seemed a more acceptable line of reasoning to feed the people which would obscure their real objections to the presence of Jesus Christ.

The people sensed an underlying tension which motivated the leaders and which, if expressed, would defeat their purpose and render them hypocrites and irrelevant. So the question is asked: *"Do the rulers know indeed that this is the very Christ?"* Could it be that they know a truth which they would rather keep hidden from the knowledge of the common man? Again, to answer that question truthfully would authenticate Christ and render them dishonest. They had for the longest while sought to discredit Christ, so they just could not afford an about face which would undoubtedly suppress them into oblivion while at the same time propel Christ into the lime light. Their very survival depended on perpetuating a lie even to the destruction of the people whom they sought to represent. Pet beliefs are sometimes the excuse that we proffer although there are constant nagging suspicions that we may be wrong.

The Scriptures say of them, and to many today, *"But woe unto you, Scribes and Pharisees, hypocrites! For ye shut up the kingdom of heaven against men: for ye neither go in yourselves, neither suffer ye them that are entering to go in." (Matt.23:13).* Because they did not want to lose their following they did not allow others to benefit from the truth. The result is that they were perishing and they caused others to perish also. In many instances they used doubt to cause mistrust and sometimes used downright prohibitions. People seem to be more comfortable with the familiar and are reluctant to move to the new. That disposition served the purpose of the Scribes and Pharisees well. Under such conditions they would maintain the status quo.

A little knowledge is a dangerous thing. The Jews fell into that trap with their next statement. *"Howbeit we know this man whence he is: but when Christ cometh, no man knoweth whence he is". (Jn. 7:27).* Jesus had fallen into the category of the familiar home town boy. "We know Him"! Having been raised in Nazareth seemed to be a disadvantage to Jesus Christ. Many were familiar with most of His historical background and therefore concluded that His history did not lend itself to their expectations of the Christ. They were familiar with His perceived "lacks" and "failures". Even if there were no negatives that could be said against Him but the mere fact that 'we watched Him grow up', speaks volumes. 'We interacted with Him daily. We did not see anything spectacular or outstanding in that child that would command awe and admiration or even raise the speculation of whether He was more than a mere man. We would have seen or heard...'

Further, there were preconceived notions of what the Christ perhaps might do or say. They might have had thoughts that He would appear from nowhere and just be a superstar from the word go. So they continued their thoughts: *"But when Christ cometh, no man knoweth whence he is" (Jn.*

*7:27).* Their Christ might appear as a grown man. Their generalizations allowed for a grand entrance which would take the country by storm, making headlines in every local and international tabloid but not such humble beginnings as had been witnessed by them. Their generalizations even denied all that had been written about Him in the scriptures and said that no man would know whence he was. They had not recognized the magnitude of the prophecies which had been fulfilled in Him since His birth. They even surmised that since they knew Him from a little child in Nazareth, that he had been born there. They did not realize all the news catching incidents which had surrounded His birth and infancy; the fact that so many little children had lost their lives because Herod wanted to be sure that he did not miss that special child – he that was born King of the Jews - in his dragnet. They had missed His epic first reading in the synagogue in Nazareth where He read the Scriptures and applied its meaning to Himself; how the elders had sought to throw Him over the cliff but He had slipped through their hands to safety. Their self-proclaimed knowledge proved to be their undoing.

Jesus, in pandering to their "knowledge", did concede that they knew Him and of course where He came from. What they did not know was that He did not come of Himself. They had knowledge of his earthly existence but had no knowledge of His heavenly origin and purpose. He was here on a mission and unless He revealed that to them they would have no knowledge of His purpose.

Jesus further declared that the one who had sent Him was true. That reminds one of the exchanges between Jesus and Pilate regarding truth. Jesus seemed again to be provoking the thought that there are common beliefs among men but there is a truth. That truth resided in and with Him. He did declare, "I am the truth" – a statement which confounded His hearers including His disciples.

The third claim by Jesus in the passage under consideration is that the Jews did not know who had sent Him, but He, Jesus, knew Him. That was a personal knowledge borne out of familiarity through an eternal co-existence. He had shared a glory with the Father which had been temporarily set aside because of the mission He had to accomplish. (Phil. 2:5 – 7; cf. Jn. 17:5).

Many who heard Jesus speak and saw the miracles that He did believed on Him contrary to the expectations of their religious leaders. His works had testified to His claims that he had come in fulfillment of their Old Testament prophecy in Isaiah 61:1, 2:

> *The spirit of the Lord GOD is upon me; because the LORD hath anointed me to preach good tidings unto the meek; he hath sent me to bind up the brokenhearted, to proclaim liberty to the captives, and the opening of the prison to them that are bound; To proclaim the acceptable year of the LORD."*

Those who had heard the defamation of Jesus Christ by the religious leaders had a very penetrating question for their leaders: *"And many of the people believed on him, and said, When Christ cometh, will he do more miracles than these which this man hath done?"* (Jn. 7:31)

Even today mankind is deceived into believing that the facts concerning Jesus are continually being developed until ultimately there will be a Jesus that is consistent with the beliefs of man. A not-so-old survey of the American Christian population revealed that despite the records of the Bible there are numerous inconsistencies and downright contradictions among proclaimed adherents. A Bob Unruh report of a Barna Group Poll states: "Half of Americans who call themselves "Christian" don't believe Satan exists and fully one-third are confident that Jesus sinned while on Earth."[21]

These are two fundamental truths of the Holy Scriptures being violated by the seeming knowledge of these Christians. Not only does the Bible tell us who Satan is, but it tells us where He came from and what His mission is. Jesus, Himself, in speaking of the Devil, who is also Satan and the Prince of this World, confirms both truths when he says: *"Hereafter I will not talk much with you: for the prince of this world cometh, and hath nothing in me."* (John 14:30) His reference to the Devil acknowledges his existence. His statement that "(he) hath nothing in me" establishes the sinlessness of Christ's life. For Jesus to speak a lie here would make him an adherent of Satan who is the father of lies. *"Ye are of your father the devil, and the lusts of your father ye will do. He was a murderer from the beginning, and abode not in the truth, because there is no truth in him. When he speaketh a lie, he speaketh of his own: for he is a liar, and the father of it."* (Jn. 8:44) Even in that case He would still be ascertaining the existence of Satan. But Jesus Christ is true – the exact opposite of what Satan is.

The report continues to highlight the following misconceptions of some who call themselves Christian:

"Americans are increasingly comfortable picking and choosing what they deem to be helpful and accurate theological views and have become comfortable discarding the rest of the teachings in the Bible,"[22] he said.

Barna noted the millions of people who describe themselves as Christian and believe Jesus sinned, or those who say they will experience eternal salvation because they confessed their sins and accepted Christ as their savior, "but also believe that a person can do enough good works to earn eternal salvation."[23] For the study, "born-again Christians" were defined as people who said they had made a personal commitment to Jesus Christ...

"....Christianity is just one of many options that Americans choose from and that a huge majority of adults pick and choose what they believe rather than adopt a church or denomination's slate of beliefs."[24]

"In contrast, the poll showed the importance of belief was growing along with the number of options about what to believe."[25]

The result "underscored the fact that people no longer look to denominations or churches to offer a slate of theological views that the individual adopts in its entirety,"[26] the report said.

By a margin of 71 percent to 26 percent adults "noted that they are personally more likely to develop their own set of religious beliefs than to accept a comprehensive set of beliefs taught by a particular church,"[27] the report said.

"Today, Americans are more likely to pit a variety of non-Christian options against various Christian-based views. This has resulted in an abundance of unique worldviews based on personal combinations of theology drawn from a smattering of world religions such as Christianity, Buddhism, Judaism, Hinduism, and Islam as well as secularism."[28]

Another fib which is rampant among some is that Jesus will never return to this sin cursed earth again. He was here once and was so ill-treated that He left leaving man to his own. He will not come back to be ill-treated by man again. This particular belief reflects a misunderstanding of who Christ is, the facts concerning His life on earth, the purpose for His return, and the power with which He will return.

Not without significance is the popular concept of who Christ is in Christianity; that simply the use of His name is a ticket into heaven. The story which Jesus told of the rich man and Lazarus should dispel the many deceptions in Christian circles as featured in the story.

One of the first is the use of the name and acknowledgement of God as 'Father'. In this instance Abraham stands out as representing the Father. The rich man calls out to Him from hell. What a contradiction! Your father, yet you are in hell? Many will find themselves in such a predicament after death when they realize that although they had named the name of God, their lives had not been consistent with their claims. God cannot be your father while you live for the Devil. Saying that we serve the same God and use the same Bible does not constitute salvation. Many may even claim having done particular works in His name but would not be recognized by the Lord.

Many will say to me in that day,

> *Lord, Lord, have we not prophesied in thy name? And in thy name have cast out devils? And in thy name done many wonderful works? And then will I profess unto them, I never knew you: depart from me, ye that work iniquity* (Matt. 7:22, 23).

The inherent knowledge which many claim to have is at best faulty. The Scriptures declare: *"The heart is deceitful above all things, and desperately wicked: who can know it?"* (Jer. 17:9). One's dependence on a depraved heart is dangerous. Its basic characteristic is deception.

Jesus had some scathing remarks for the religious leaders of His day. Many today fall into the same category of those learned leaders. They had the zeal, they had the form, they had some knowledge, but they fell miserably short of God's standards. Christ said this to them:

> *"But woe unto you, scribes and Pharisees, hypocrites! For ye shut up the kingdom of heaven against men: for ye neither go in yourselves, neither suffer ye them that are entering to go in."*

*"Woe unto you, scribes and Pharisees, hypocrites! for ye compass sea and land to make one proselyte, and when he is made, ye make him twofold more the child of hell than yourselves"* (Matt. 23:13, 15).

In effect the Jews were busy converting others to Judaism (the Jewish religion) making proselytes (disciples, converts) of them. One would have thought that with their conversion these Jewish disciples would have been more prone to understanding Jesus Christ. Christ's evaluation of them was that they had become twice more the children of hell than they were before. One would think this an impossibility, but experience has shown that this is a reality. Paul in his missionary journeys encountered both Jews, his countrymen, and Jewish proselytes who opposed the message of the Gospel (Acts 13, and 14). Indeed, one needs not go so far for such opposition was the cause of the arrest of the Apostles and the murder of James (Acts 3, 4, 12). The reality is that persons are more difficult to convince of the truth once they have accepted a deception which they hold as true.

### The Witness of John the Baptist:

John the Baptist was one of the most down to earth ambassadors who testified of Jesus Christ. He had never met the man and had admitted as much to his hearers. John had been commissioned to perform a duty and he accepted his responsibility with all vigor and zeal. He marched into the arena of public opinion armed only with the assurance that when the time was right he would recognize the one of whom he spake. One thing John was assured of was that he was a forerunner of one who was to come and that this great person could possibly be in their midst even as he spoke. A second thing John was assured of was that this person whom he represented was great and that he paled in comparison to His greatness. John was unabashed in his pronouncements and did not apologize for his lack of more detail. John declared of that coming person: *"whose shoe's latchet I am not worthy to unloose"* (John 1:27).

John had much to say in the line of publicizing and promoting the coming of that important personality but had no illusions regarding either his priorities or his role. He readily identified himself as the forerunner of the one who was to come. He proudly proclaims, *"I am the voice of one crying in the wilderness, make straight the way of the Lord as said the prophet Esaias"* (John 1:23). His quotation from the Prophet Isaiah indicated that the one he preceded was the long awaited Messiah of the Jews. The Jews had lived with the expectation of a coming Messiah and had wondered at the advent of John. They were ready to accept him because he seemed to fit their concept of the kind of entry befitting such a prestigious personality. But John said otherwise.

Because John had not accepted their acclaim they questioned his actions. *"Why then do you baptize if you are not that Christ, nor Elias, neither that prophet?"* (Jn. 1:25). Such baptism signaled to them the beginning of a new movement which they might have identified with. Even the Romans accepted his preaching and readily identified with the new movement (Lk. 3:14). But John pointed to another baptism which only that special one could administer. Not only was the baptism superior but the person administering would be much more superior. John says, *"He it is, who coming after me is preferred before me, whose shoe's latchet I am not worthy to unloose"* (John 1:27).

John had keys that would identify the Christ. The first key was wrapped up in the purpose for which John came baptizing. He says, *"And I knew him not: but that he should be made manifest to Israel, therefore am I come baptizing with water"* (Jn. 1:31). Jesus would be identified to Him during and through the process of baptism. Jesus, indeed, was recognized by John. But did Israel recognize their Christ?

The second key was the testimony of God. God bore witness to the authenticity of Jesus Christ when the Spirit descended upon Him as a dove. John also remarks that this was one of the identifying marks, since He had no previous knowledge of who the Christ was.

> *And John bare record, saying, I saw the Spirit descending from heaven like a dove, and it abode upon him. And I knew him not: but he that sent me to baptize with water, the same said unto me, <u>Upon whom thou shalt see the Spirit descending, and remaining on him, the same is he which baptizeth with the Holy Ghost</u>. And I saw, and bare record that this is the Son of God* (Jn. 1:32 - 34). (underline mine)

In the Gospel of Matthew we have further information that along with the Spirit descending upon Jesus there was a voice from heaven declaring, *"This is my beloved Son, in whom I am well pleased."* Unmistakably and undeniably, Jesus was the awaited Christ. Not only was He the Christ but He was Emmanuel - God come in the flesh.

Because God had identified the Christ to Him, John was now able to point to Jesus and direct the people to Him. It was then he was able to say, *"Behold the Lamb of God which taketh away the sin of the world"* (Jn. 1:29).

## John's Doubts:

Not too long ago John had so eloquently and dynamically introduced Jesus as the promised Messiah, the Christ. He had termed Him "the Lamb of God which taketh away the sin of the world." Now John is in prison for rebuking Herod for having his brother's wife. Not having the freedom to move about, John only hears of the things which Jesus did. That of itself should have signaled to John that Jesus was indeed the Christ. John now sends to Jesus to enquire whether he was the Christ or whether they should look for another.

That should have been disheartening to Jesus. After such a bold introduction - a question like this? But Christ understood the quandary of John. His query had less to do with the identity of Christ and more to do with John's present situation. John must have surmised that with the power and authority of Jesus he should be out of prison. Being so restricted allowed him time to reflect on himself and his predicament. Why should that be?

Jesus on the other hand, with much diplomacy and care gave a public demonstration in the presence of John's disciples. As He had read from the book of Isaiah 61:1, 2 sometime previously, He demonstrates the things which would characterize the one who should come. The blind received their sight; the lame walked, the lepers were cleansed; the deaf were made to hear and even the dead were brought back to life. This was the mission of the Christ and that was demonstrated in their presence. Jesus now directs John's disciples to go back to John and tell what they had seen.

In the absence of John's disciples, Jesus proceeds to vindicate John. With masterful rhetorical questions he directs the thinking of his audience to the real person whom they had experienced in the Jordan River. He had not been a push over kind of guy neither was he a suave, smooth talker from the city. Instead his role had been admirably acted out and earned him the high accolades that he was the greatest among the prophets. That was demonstrated in his having the distinguished honor of being the forerunner of the Christ.

**The Testimony of Jesus Christ:**

One readily accepts the concept that in the mouth of two or three witnesses every word shall be established. In actual fact this principle comes from God Himself. This was one of the policies that the Jewish Deity instituted which had application in both their religious and civil lives. It is one that the legal system today partially subscribes to. One cannot be convicted simply on the testimony of one. The Old Testament states:

> *So these things shall be for a statute of judgment unto you throughout your generations in all your dwellings. Whoso killeth any person, the murderer shall be put to death by the mouth of witnesses: but one witness shall not testify against any person to cause him to die* (Nu. 35:29, 30).

> *Then shalt thou bring forth that man or that woman, which have committed that wicked thing, unto thy gates, even that man or that woman, and shalt stone them with stones, till they die. At the mouth of two witnesses, or three witnesses, shall he that is worthy of death be put to death; but at the mouth of one witness he shall not be put to death* (Deut. 17:5, 6).

The same sentiment is echoed in the New Testament:

> *Moreover if thy brother shall trespass against thee, go and tell him his fault between thee and him alone: if he shall hear thee, thou hast gained thy brother. But if he will not hear thee, then take with thee one or two more, that in the mouth of two or three witnesses every word may be established* (Mt. 18:15, 16).

Careful consideration of the life and teachings of Christ would reveal that, like God, it was a difficult proposition to verify or authenticate Him. The only persons who could certify the truthfulness of the claims of Christ were God and the Devil. God was unseen and was difficult to accept. But His works spoke to His existence and power. The Devil would not readily testify because it was not in his best interest to do so. His demons, however, once attempted to testify of who Christ was but Christ rejected their testimony.

> *And when he was come to the other side into the country of the Gergesenes, there met him two possessed with devils, coming out of the tombs, exceeding fierce, so that no man might pass by that way. And, behold, they cried out, saying, 'What have we to do with thee, Jesus, thou Son of God? Art thou come hither to torment us before the time?'* (Matt. 8:28, 29).

## They knew who Jesus was:

Jesus' disciples, too, had difficulty accepting fully all that their Master had said. To them Jesus appealed not only to His words, but also to the works He had done in their presence for testimony. To their request to see the Father, Jesus said:

> *...Have I been so long time with you, and yet hast thou not known me, Philip? He that hath seen me hath seen the Father; and how sayest thou then, Show us the Father? Believest thou not that I am in the Father, and the Father in me? The words that I speak unto you I speak not of myself: but the Father that dwelleth in me, he doeth the works. Believe me that I am in the Father, and the Father in me: or else*

*believe me for the very works' sake* (Jn. 14:9-11). *(underline mine)*

Jesus, who was God in the flesh, had the same identity problem as God the Father and was entitled to the same standard of measurement as the Father. To His friend Abraham in the Old Testament, God found it necessary to authenticate Himself on a human level. He adopted a human practice in order to convince His friend Abraham of the surety of the covenant made with him. The Bible records:

*And the angel of the LORD called unto Abraham out of heaven the second time, And said, 'By myself have I sworn, saith the LORD, for because thou hast done this thing, and hast not withheld thy son, thine only son: That in blessing I will bless thee, and in multiplying I will multiply thy seed as the stars of the heaven, and as the sand which is upon the sea shore; and thy seed shall possess the gate of his enemies; and in thy seed shall all the nations of the earth be blessed; because thou hast obeyed my voice' ( Gen. 22;15 -18).*

*For men verily swear by the greater: and an oath for confirmation is to them an end of all strife. Wherein God, willing more abundantly to show unto the heirs of promise the immutability of his counsel, confirmed it by an oath: that by two immutable things, in which it was impossible for God to lie, we might have a strong consolation, who have fled for refuge to lay hold upon the hope set before us:* (Heb. 6:16 – 18).

God had His Divine character of truthfulness on the line and to that He added the human element of swearing.

We have very forceful evidence of the divinity of Jesus Christ in that He claimed equality with God the Father. When we accept the nature of God we must in like manner accept the veracity of Jesus Christ.

Jesus did not only appeal to His words and miracles for authentication of His identity, but to the challenge of the Jewish leadership He responded accordingly:

> *Then answered the Jews and said unto him, What sign showest thou unto us, seeing that thou doest these things?*
>
> *Jesus answered and said unto them, 'Destroy this temple, and in three days I will raise it up'.*
>
> *Then said the Jews, 'Forty and six years was this temple in building, and wilt thou rear it up in three days'?*
>
> *But he spake of the temple of his body. When, therefore, he was risen from the dead, his disciples remembered that he had said this unto them; and they believed the scripture, and the word which Jesus had said. Now when he was in Jerusalem at the Passover, in the feast day, many believed in his name, when they saw the miracles which he did* (Jn. 2:18 – 23).

This was at the very beginning of His ministry which lasted three and a half years among the Jews. Jesus here predicts His death and resurrection as authentication of His identity. There could not be a greater response to the queries of His detractors. Although it would wait for a period of time, His eventual death and resurrection sealed up the question regarding His identity. The fact that He could predict such a powerful event in His life years beforehand speaks to a divine quality of foreknowledge. In time He also informed them that no man takes His life from Him. He lays it down at will and takes it up again at will. What greater proof of His power could there be than that He as a dead man could take back His life?

> 'Therefore doth my Father love me, because I lay down my life, that I might take it again. No man taketh it from me, but I lay it down of myself. I have power to lay it down, and I have power to take it again. This commandment have I received of my Father'.
>
> There was a division therefore again among the Jews for these sayings. And many of them said, He hath a devil, and is mad; why hear ye him? (Jn. 10:17 – 20).

The immediate effects of his resurrection were amazing. One would have thought that at that point that, if his claims were at all frivolous, the crowds would have known and that its reality could have been successfully challenged. Producing the body would have dispelled any notions floating around the grapevines. Again what sane person would commit his life to such a "falsehood" just at the time when that could have been disproven? The records reveal that although Christ had made His claims which indeed were truth, that even His disciples harbored some skepticism until the time of the event. Seeing the risen Christ answered it all for both His disciples and other witnesses of the resurrection. Thomas, one of Christ's disciples, was not convinced until he was confronted and invited to thrust his hands into the wounds which Christ had sustained during his trial and crucifixion. Not only did Christ rise from the dead but he also allowed many other dead people to rise and walk the streets of Jerusalem as testimony that the dead do rise and that Christ had power over death. Is not this the Christ?

The resurrection of Lazarus mere days before had heightened their expectations of a resurrection. That phenomenon had presented irrefutable proof that Christ indeed had power to raise the dead. Lazarus' resurrection had not been on the day of his death but four days later ensuring that not only had he been dead but also that all physical steps had been taken to remove the dead corpse out of their sight. Christ had not been present so He had not influenced the putting away of the dead. The accusations of the sisters show that their expectations had seemingly been devastatingly flouted. Their anticipations at informing Him of the sickness of their brother had flagged and now rested in the hope that one day in the future, in another life, they would see their brother again. They had no misgivings concerning their immediate letdown as indicated by the conversation between Jesus and Martha. But Christ raised Lazarus from the dead.

Ah!! But you say the whole thing was a setup. You had to have been there to experience the frustrations and anxiety of the religious leaders as they contemplated what to do with the evidence that stared them in the face. That was added motivation to want to remove Jesus from among them. The evidence – Lazarus – would summarily be dealt with also so that there would be no sign of the miracle that had taken place. It was against that backdrop that Jesus allowed Himself to be taken and slain so that He would not only prove His claims but also deal with the sin problem which confronted mankind. Had even the Devil and his operatives known the result of their seeming triumph they would not have sought the death of Christ. Even in their contemplated act of wickedness they were active participants in the greatest victory that Christ came to accomplish.

> *Therefore doth my Father love me, because I lay down my life, that I might take it again. No man taketh it from me, but I lay it down of myself. I have power to lay it down, and I have power to take it again. This commandment have I received of my Father* (Jn. 10:17, 18).

How many or who of the other religious leaders has performed such a feat? Recording such events before they happen alone is phenomenal. Hearing them and seeing them come to pass is overwhelming. Some may claim that these were self-fulfilling prophecies but what about the many prophecies fulfilled that were written years before over a wide range of time by so many different writers who in some cases knew nothing of each other or their writings? What about the prophecies which were fulfilled at His birth and leading up to His birth; about the place of His birth; local events at the time of His birth; the sudden appearance of the shepherds; their expressed source of information regarding the birth of the child? What about the visit of the Magi from so far away; the legally chronicled record of Herod's infamous act of genocide of infants less than two years seeking to erase the threat to his kingdom that Jesus had no physical means of affecting as a human? Despite such overwhelming proof, some today still deny the very existence of Jesus Christ. History could not be more demonstrative of the historicity of Jesus Christ. Our very calendars are reckoned relative to His existence.

Christ is no imposter; He existed and His claims are verifiable. Ask Josephus, the local Jewish historian. Though he had not witnessed the events personally, the prevalent stories which continued for years following were recorded to leave no doubt that they had transpired. The Apostle Paul, who, days before, had been an agnostic, had converted and had become a proponent of the facts of the resurrection. In one such account he points to the fact that a group of over five hundred people had witnessed Jesus after His resurrection and was in most cases still alive at the time of his writing. They could easily disprove his story if it were not true (I Cor.15:6).

There has been a historic Christ.

# CHAPTER THREE

# THE GOD FACTOR

It is interesting that there should be a discussion regarding the existence of God, but it becomes necessary because of the preponderance of arguments for and against the subject. It would seem that just the frequency with which the subject recurs, makes it necessary that there be a God and if per chance one did not exist one should be created. Of course the antagonist would argue equally vehemently that there should not be one, the simple reason being that the existence of one would upset his entire philosophy of life and his daily routine. The thought of a god takes away ones presumed independence and assumed mastery over his surroundings. To say that there is a god would make one accountable to him and accountable in areas which one would rather not be. To admit that there is a god allows for a supreme who designed. "Random selection" or "the survival of the fittest" would dissipate if there were a god. One's reliance in one's innate abilities would give way to dependency upon a supreme.

Equally interesting is the prevalence of a god in the lives of the many societies that map our planet. Every society embraces the thought of a supreme being. To that end there were artifacts created to represent that one who is not seen.

There were assigned places considered sacred or consecrated to the worship of such an one. Researchers have excavated and found that, especially in areas indicated by the Holy Scriptures, there have been numerous forms of worship as reflected by the findings. For what it's worth, historically, a god has existed in the minds of people. Without a god, there is no religion. Conversely, since there is religion, there is of necessity a god. The questions then arise: "Who is He?" "Is He knowable?" "Where can He be found?"

The Bible does not entertain an explanation of God in its introduction but simply declares His existence as the source of all else. God does not explain His origin because He has none. His presence at the time of creation presupposes His pre-existence to the things which He created. *"In the beginning God created the heavens and the earth"* (Gen. 1:1).

God goes to lengths to declare His existence. *"The heavens declare the glory of God and the firmament showeth His handiwork"* (Psalm 19:1). In like manner as the earth is surrounded with our atmosphere and indeed the universe, God has left evidence of His existence. These very things which we see around us are testimony of His existence. His creative power is evident throughout the universe, for surely, such elaborate layout of heavenly bodies could no more come into being by chance than anyone of man's inventions just happening. There had to be a mastermind. Nothing came into existence without His saying so. The passage of scripture continues to bear out the fact that God exists. It says that the phenomena of day and night are testimony of the existence of God.

> *Day unto day uttereth speech, and night unto night showeth knowledge. There is no speech nor language, where their voice is not heard. Their line is gone out through all the earth, and their words to the end of the world. In them hath he set a tabernacle for*

*the sun, which is as a bridegroom coming out of his chamber, and rejoiceth as a strong man to run a race* (Ps. 19:2-5).

God further indicts man in that He has both declared Himself visibly and intellectually to man. Nature screams out that there is a designer with intelligence and profound appreciation for beauty and order. The regularity of day and night, the predictability of our seasons, the cycle of our precipitation, the fixedness of our planet earth, both in its orbit and revolution, the balance in our atmospheric conditions, the angle of our earth on its axis all shout out profoundly – design. The intricacies of the human body and the functions of each organ call for design. The coordination and cooperation of the functions of the organs of the body call for a designer. The location of the parts of the body relative to their functions was not the result of an accident neither was it by chance. Why is it that each normal human being who comes into the world comes with the same type and quantity of organs and all positioned and functioning in the same way regardless of their ethnicity or color? Why is there not differing stages of evolution within any particular specie of plant or animal life since things are supposedly constantly evolving? The cycle of life and the interdependence of living things upon each other for survival indicate there is a designer. The ability of each living thing to sustain itself by converting available matter into necessary nutrients is testimony of a supreme. Despite creation's interdependence yet each entity maintains its own identity and reproduces after its kind. One does not become what it consumes, rather what is consumed becomes a part of what consumed it.

The innate intelligence in man confirms that he was created in the image of his creator. Man's ability to understand and to follow trends reveals a uniqueness which could only come from another intelligent being. The power of reason and projection did not just happen; they are the deliberate acts of One who seeks to identify Himself and expects to be understood. The denial of these facts elicited the following remark from God regarding the ingratitude of man:

> *For the wrath of God is revealed from heaven against all ungodliness and unrighteousness of men, who hold the truth in unrighteousness; because that which may be known of God is manifest in them; for God hath showed it unto them. For the invisible things of him from the creation of the world are clearly seen, being understood by the things that are made, even his eternal power and Godhead; so that they are without excuse* (Rom. 1:18 – 20).

Man is endowed with knowledge of the Supreme. Not only is the knowledge of God built into the being of man, his surroundings reveal God in ways that are recognizable and understandable. Creation exudes power and infinite knowledge. Until now, man has not fathomed the wealth of information contained in his immediate surroundings. Despite this fact, man cherishes the thought of defying God and denying His very existence.

Man's actions carried serious consequences. His rejection of declared observable truth rendered him a fool. Man's present condition is not a "factory fault" but a deliberate act of rebellion against what was known. The Bible tells us in Romans 1:22 "…he became…" This indicates a change from what was, to what is. His present condition was generated from an attitude which was not inherent but one acquired over time. The Bible further reveals the source of the corruption in man's constitution and his ultimate self-destruction. The wicked one has done this. He seeks recognition for himself and attempts to get it by corrupting the creation of God. What God desired was worship from his creatures so the devil seeks to divert that worship from the only rational being that God created to himself. He cannot get creation to be subject to him in worship but he violates the creature who alone among God's creation has volition causing him by default to worship him. "...*Whomsoever you yield yourself servants to obey, his servants you are...* " (Rom. 6:16)

But God is knowable. He was properly known before and continues to be known by those who would be obedient to Him. Many today claim that God cannot be comprehended. Consequently, man philosophizes and conjures every other thing to worship but God. It is Geisler who says, "God is an absolute paradox to man not simply because of the inability of the human mind but because of the depravity of the human heart."[29] God, through the prophet Jeremiah says, *"The heart is deceitful above all things and desperately wicked: who can know it?"* (Jer. 17:9).

## The existence of God - Why the continuous dispute?

One can ask the question regarding the ongoing debate over the existence of God. Why the debate? One accepts it as fact that God does exist and the other that He doesn't, using seemingly rational questions to create the impression that God is not possible. One simple such argument is the prevalence of hunger in some areas of the world. There are numerous responses to this question none of which ascribes blame to God. But the detractors would argue that if there were a God, why does He allow it? The debate rages on simply because there is need for a definitive answer regarding the existence and nature of God. This is so because, if there were to be a God, there are prescribed parameters to His sphere of operations. But who determines those spheres?

God, in order to be God, would have to be an absolute being. There must be neither limit to His power, nor to His knowledge, nor to his sphere of operation. Indeed it is so. Despite man's disbelief, God declares of Himself:

> *Seek ye the LORD while he may be found, call ye upon him while he is near: Let the wicked forsake his way, and the unrighteous man his thoughts: and let him return unto the LORD, and he will have mercy upon him; and to our God, for he will abundantly pardon. For my thoughts are not your thoughts, neither are your ways my ways, saith the LORD. For as the heavens are higher than the earth, so are my ways higher than your ways, and my thoughts than your thoughts* (Isa. 55:6 – 9).

God's first plea is for the faithless to abandon his disbelief and seek after Him. The challenge is that God can be found but that only while He is available. The reason for this is that God makes Himself available now, but will not always forebear the disparaging of detractors indefinitely. Because it is obvious that man's lack of knowledge of God is not for want of evidence but because of deliberate, willful ignorance. More damning is man's preposterous presumption that God can be reduced to the sphere of his finite mind. There is great disparity between the thoughts of God and those of man. There is equally great disproportion between the ways of God and those of man. God's contrast (not comparison) is that "as the heavens are higher than the earth" so is the gulf which exists between the intelligence of man and that of his God. In simple terms God's thoughts and God's ways are infinitely different from those of man with God's attributes far more superior to those of man. God concludes, therefore, as He said to the Children of Israel, *"And ye shall seek me, and find me, when ye shall search for me with all your heart"* (Jer. 29:13.).

## The need for a God:

As has been seen by the continuous dispute, there must be a need for God or the dispute is futile. Several questions present themselves begging for rational answers which seem to spawn further questions, the only logical answer being that there must of necessity be a God.

One such question is, "Why are so many claiming to be something that is non-existent?" From the earliest records of man's history there have been claims and impersonations of an entity which according to our 'wise' of today does not exist. Does that concept redound to the level of ignorance and/or superstition of man? Or does it account for the fact that man knows that he is accountable to a supreme being and that the denial is a feeble attempt to rid himself of guilt and responsibility?

Coupled with the belief and impersonations is also the high level of idols and idol worship that we have in the world. One may argue that this is a spinoff of the misconceptions discussed previously, but even that, too, has longstanding historical roots. Why the perpetuation of such "known myths"? The word of God makes light of such practices in ways that make the adherents look ridiculous and any wise person considering these jeers would discontinue his affiliations. Consider the manufacturing of these gods out of lifeless material such as stone and clay. These would not move on their own volition but must be moved by their owners. The same is true of those made of wood. As the Bible remarks, part of the wood is used to make that god and the remainder is used to burn as fuel. This is not a phenomenon among the unlearned peasantry only but one which extends to the very throne of nations. The major religions of today with all their educated adherents and sophistication continue to worship in the presence of idols claiming that these are mere reminders of the presence of

God. The need for worship and a representation of a deity to accompany such worship seem to be intrinsic in man and not a mere outward performance of fluff.

The Bible speaks of a time coming when there will be one who will impersonate the Christ. He will perform miracles which will deceive many because this will fulfill their expectations of what a God should be able to do. More than that, the sight of such miracles will be undeniable because in our day of mass communication, the activities will be digitally recorded and transmitted around the world in an instant. The fact of impersonating God and His Christ is not farfetched because even now man is looking for one such super leader who will be able to take control of the world economically and politically and bring about a form of unity which will resolve all the world's ills. This is discussed globally and referred to as the New World Order. Why the need for a single person to control the world and not allow individual countries to mind their own affairs? Alongside the Antichrist will be another super leader who will unite the world religiously. Should that not be a grand occasion to do away with everything religious since it is a myth and, of course, a New World Order will be in existence? There will be unified religion because there is cognitive awareness that there is a supreme.

Evolution, today's new answer-all 'religion', presents another enigma for agnostics. One of the things that evolution has the most of is time. Time is necessary to allow for the development of everything apparent or existent. Time made it possible for the progression from stage to stage and state to state of all which exist today. Despite the fact that millions and sometimes billions of years were necessary, these were available to allow for the life forms that we have today to come into being. But where or when did time begin? Along with the theory of cause and effect one can build layers of causes resulting in the effects that we see around us today. How did the co-ordination of these begin to allow for today's level of development?

One cannot argue a previous cause ad infinitum. There must have been something or someone to start off the processes that we observe around us. Regardless of the length of time thought necessary for our sophisticated world with all its intricacies to develop, there must have been a starting point. That starting point is what makes it so necessary that there be a god. Someone, somewhere, must have started the motions which have resulted in our existence. We cannot deny our own existence as a mirage or a blob because there is such organization and constancy in us that we are recognizable beings and not mere illusions. If we were illusions what would account for the constancy and consistency of individuals far removed from each other by parentage, nationality and time (years of lifetime) which would allow for trustworthy research necessary and available for the maintenance of the physical health of the body? There must of necessity be a god.

One other unanswered question in evolution which requires our attention is the origin of time. We seem to have taken it as a given that time always existed. But where did it all begin? Did time simply jump into existence out of nothing? Why was it so necessary for there to be time which would allow for evolution? Who determined that time was the factor which was most necessary? It is more possible and plausible that there is an "uncaused cause"[30] who brought about all that is observable (and unseen) around us than to accept that these things just happened.

## Jesus Christ revealed God:

Regardless of what one may think of Jesus Christ, the fact that He existed is undeniable. There have been so much said regarding Christ that He is inescapable. It has been said that history is His story. The calculation of time is intricately woven into his life that the years before Him are calculated as B.C. and since then as A.D (in the year of Our Lord). Since it is nigh impossible to do away with the fact that Christ existed, it may be just as difficult to do away with the thought of God the Father since Jesus had so much to say of Him. *No man hath seen God at any time; the only begotten Son, which is in the bosom of the Father, he hath declared him* (Jn. 1:18).

> *In the beginning was the Word, and the Word was with God, and the Word was God. The same was in the beginning with God. All things were made by him; and without him was not any thing made that was made.*
>
> *And the Word was made flesh, and dwelt among us, (and we beheld his glory, the glory as of the only begotten of the Father,) full of grace and truth* (Jn. 1:1-3, 14).

While Christ only became known publicly from birth He pre-existed His birth. As the preceding passages of Scripture inform us - He created, therefore, He pre-exists creation. It is this same creator who became flesh and was known to us as Jesus Christ. It is He who the angel declared to Joseph should be called Jesus and would be known as Emmanuel (God with us) (Matt. 1:21, 23).

> *And she shall bring forth a son, and thou shalt call his name JESUS: for he shall save his people from their sins. Now all this was done, that it might be fulfilled which was spoken of the Lord by the prophet, saying, behold, a virgin shall be with child, and shall bring forth a son, and they shall call his name*

*Emmanuel, which being interpreted is, God with us*
(Matt. 1:21-23).

## Jesus' continuous reference to the Father:

Throughout the Gospels, which record the life and ministry of Jesus on earth, we have direct statements and quotations of Jesus regarding His Father. In the Gospel of John alone we have reference made to "The Father" or "My Father" about thirty-eight times. Examples of this can be found in these few references: Jn. 2:16; 5:17: 6:43; 8:38. A direct reference and correlation between Jesus Christ and God is found in the claim of Christ which says:

*My Father, which gave them me, is greater than all; and no man is able to pluck them out of my Father's hand. I and my Father are one* (Jn. 10:29-30).

Jesus Christ thus associated the reality and existence of the Father to His own. If Christ did not exist then God does not exist. Since Christ existed (even today we have all indication of this) then God existed. Since Christ established His eternality then that of God is also established.

*Jesus answered, If I honour myself, my honour is nothing: it is my Father that honoureth me; of whom ye say, that he is your God: yet ye have not known him; but I know him: and if I should say, I know him not, I shall be a liar like unto you: but I know him, and keep his saying.*
*Your father Abraham rejoiced to see my day: and he saw it, and was glad. Then said the Jews unto him, Thou art not yet fifty years old, and hast thou seen Abraham?*

*Jesus said unto them, Verily, verily, I say unto you, 'Before Abraham was, I am.'*

*Then took they up stones to cast at him: but Jesus hid himself, and went out of the temple, going through the midst of them, and so passed by* (Jn. 8:54-59).

*These words spake Jesus, and lifted up his eyes to heaven, and said, Father, the hour is come; glorify thy Son, that thy Son also may glorify thee: as thou hast given him power over all flesh, that he should give eternal life to as many as thou hast given him.*

*And this is life eternal, that they might know thee the only true God, and Jesus Christ, whom thou hast sent. I have glorified thee on the earth: I have finished the work which thou gavest me to do.*

*And now, O Father, glorify thou me with thine own self with the glory which I had with thee before the world was. I have manifested thy name unto the men which thou gavest me out of the world: thine they were, and thou gavest them me; and they have kept thy word* (Jn. 17:1-6).

Any question regarding these claims should not be whether He made them or not, but whether they are true.

## Jesus is referred to as the Creator – equality with God:

In the passage quoted above (Jn. 1:1, 13-14) Jesus Christ is referred to as the Creator of the world. In Genesis 1:1 we have recorded that God created the heavens and the earth. This is no contradiction. As has been seen from a comparison of the passages discussed above, Jesus Christ is the physical representation of the God of the Old Testament. His name Emmanuel declared that. All actions attributed to

Jesus are attributable to God also. One may readily counter that it was only Jesus who died on the cross and that would be right when we regard the functions of the persons of the Godhead. But in the light of Matthew 1:21 and 23 it was God in the person of Jesus who would save His people from their sin.

In many other ways Jesus showed Himself to be God by His actions and statements. His forgiving the sins of the sick man borne by four friends elicited the comment from the Jews: *"Who can forgive sins but God alone?"*

Paul, one of the prolific writers of the New Testament, propounded the Biblical doctrine of the deity of Jesus Christ with numerous statements regarding His person and position. In his writings, too, we see many references to God as the Father and to Jesus Christ as the Son. We see references to the relationship between the two as well as the function of each. We see Christ as all-encompassing in the Godhead and His mission in the redemption and restoration of man. We see all the attributes of God manifested in the Son and His being the medium through whom the grace of God is bestowed upon men. He is the head of all principalities and powers and we are complete in Him. He is God's final emissary from heaven and the authority through whom God is going to call the world into account.

> *To the saints and faithful brethren in Christ which are at Colosse: Grace be unto you, and peace, from God our Father and the Lord Jesus Christ.. We give thanks to God and the Father of our Lord Jesus Christ, praying always for you, since we heard of your faith in Christ Jesus* (Col. 1:2-4).
>
> *Giving thanks unto the Father, which hath made us meet to be partakers of the inheritance of the saints in light: who hath delivered us from the power of darkness, and hath translated us into the kingdom of*

*his dear Son: in whom we have redemption through his blood, even the forgiveness of sins: who is the image of the invisible God, the firstborn of every creature: for by him were all things created, that are in heaven, and that are in earth, visible and invisible, whether they be thrones, or dominions, or principalities, or powers: all things were created by him, and for him: and he is before all things, and by him all things consist. And he is the head of the body, the church: who is the beginning, the firstborn from the dead; that in all things he might have the preeminence.*

*For it pleased the Father that in him should all fullness dwell; and, having made peace through the blood of his cross, by him to reconcile all things unto himself; by him, I say, whether they be things in earth, or things in heaven.* (Col 1:12-20).

*For I would that ye knew what great conflict I have for you, and for them at Laodicea, and for as many as have not seen my face in the flesh; that their hearts might be comforted, being knit together in love, and unto all riches of the full assurance of understanding, to the acknowledgment of the mystery of God, and of the Father, and of Christ; in whom are hid all the treasures of wisdom and knowledge. And this I say, lest any man should beguile you with enticing words* (Col 2:1-4).

*Beware lest any man spoil you through philosophy and vain deceit, after the tradition of men, after the rudiments of the world, and not after Christ. For in him dwelleth all the fullness of the Godhead bodily. And ye are complete in him, which is the head of all principality and power* (Col. 2:8-10).

*And all things are of God, who hath reconciled us to himself by Jesus Christ, and hath given to us the ministry of reconciliation; to wit, that God*

*was in Christ, reconciling the world unto Himself,
not imputing their trespasses unto them; and hath
committed unto us the word of reconciliation* (II
Cor5:18, 19).

*God, who at sundry times and in divers manners spake
in time past unto the fathers by the prophets, hath in
these last days spoken unto us by his Son, whom he
hath appointed heir of all things, by whom also he
made the worlds; Who being the brightness of his glory,
and the express image of his person, and upholding
all things by the word of his power, when he had by
himself purged our sins, sat down on the right hand of
the Majesty on high; being made so much better than
the angels, as he hath by inheritance obtained a more
excellent name than they* (Heb. 1:1-4).

## Jesus' declaration - seeing Him is seeing the Father:

Jesus had no qualm about His identity. He knew who
He was and He made it abundantly and unmistakably clear
that He knew who He was and that His disciples should
know also. He is co-equal with the Father and His humility
and humiliation as a man took nothing away from His
divine person.

*If ye had known me, ye should have known my
Father also: and from henceforth ye know him, and
have seen him.*

  *Philip saith unto him, Lord, show us the Father,
and it sufficeth us.*

  *Jesus saith unto him, "Have I been so long time
with you, and yet hast thou not known me, Philip?
He that hath seen me hath seen the Father; and
how sayest thou then, Show us the Father? Believest*

*thou not that I am in the Father, and the Father in me? The words that I speak unto you I speak not of myself: but the Father that dwelleth in me, he doeth the works. Believe me that I am in the Father, and the Father in me: or else believe me for the very works' sake"* (Jn. 14:7-11).

To know Jesus Christ is to know God and there should be no question of whether there is a God once we have accepted the historicity of Christ. Christ is not in isolation of the Father neither is the Father a person far removed from Christ. They are one and the same in essence though in function they carry different roles.

*Let this mind be in you, which was also in Christ Jesus: Who, being in the form of God, thought it not robbery to be equal with God: but made himself of no reputation, and took upon him the form of a servant, and was made in the likeness of men: and being found in fashion as a man, he humbled himself, and became obedient unto death, even the death of the cross; wherefore God also hath highly exalted him, and given him a name which is above every name: that at the name of Jesus every knee should bow, of things in heaven, and things in earth, and things under the earth; and that every tongue should confess that Jesus Christ is Lord, to the glory of God the Father* (Phil. 2:5-11).

# CHAPTER FOUR

# THE BIBLE - GOD'S WORD

**The claims of the Bible to be God's Word:**

The Bible claims to be God's word. Many of the writers of the multiple books of the compendium called The Holy Bible make direct claim to having spoken what had been communicated to them from and by God. The phrase "The Lord Said…" is used two hundred nineteen (219) times in the Bible. The phrase "The word of the LORD…" is used two hundred fifty (250) times in the Bible. The phrase "The word of the Lord came to…" is used twenty-seven (27) times. The word "Scripture" is used fifty-three times.

In addition to these phrases the following verses appear in the New Testament.

All Scripture…

*All scripture is given by inspiration of God, and is profitable for doctrine, for reproof, for correction, for instruction in righteousness* (II Tim. 3:16).

This is a remarkable claim made by the Bible regarding its contents. It has been seen that the word 'scripture' is used to refer to the contents of the Bible and not to all other religious books. It stands to reason that in the light of the phrases referred to above that the content of the Bible is 'all scripture'. Our verse tells us that "all scripture" is given by the inspiration of God.

It is observed, too, that although the writers were human beings the Scripture makes claim to inspiration by God. That claims a divine origin. Though men were the instruments through whom God communicated, the source of the information is God and with that inspiration comes its inerrancy, seeing that God had oversight of the original written texts. It must be said, too, that although minor discrepancies have been identified in copies of the text, God has seen to it that there has been no corruption of the information communicated.

## The claims of other scripture:

*And again another scripture saith, "They shall look on him whom they pierced" (Jn. 19:37).*

*And account that the longsuffering of our Lord is salvation; even as our beloved brother Paul also according to the wisdom given unto him hath written unto you; As also in all his epistles, speaking in them of these things; in which are some things hard to be understood, which they that are unlearned and unstable wrest, as they do also the other scriptures, unto their own destruction (II Pet 3: 15, 16).*

In referring to the rest of the Bible as compared to the writings of Paul, Peter uses the phrase "other scriptures". With his use of that phrase he authenticates the scriptures and indicates that Paul's writings are scripture. They indeed are scripture.

## God, who spoke in the past by the prophets, speaks today by Christ.

*God, who at sundry times and in divers manners spake in time past unto the fathers by the prophets, hath in these last days spoken unto us by his Son, whom he hath appointed heir of all things, by whom also he made the worlds; who being the brightness of his glory, and the express image of his person, and upholding all things by the word of his power, when he had by himself purged our sins, sat down on the right hand of the Majesty on high; being made so much better than the angels, as he hath by inheritance obtained a more excellent name than they (Heb. 1:1-4).*

Jesus quoted it:

Jesus Christ, the God-man, quoted the Old Testament Scriptures thus authenticating them. He quoted from the books of Moses (The books of the Law). He quoted from the Psalms and He quoted from the prophets. We have here a few examples of His quotations and their sources:

*But he answered and said, It is written, Man shall not live by bread alone, but by every word that proceedeth out of the mouth of God (Mt. 4:4).*

*And he humbled thee, and suffered thee to hunger, and fed thee with manna, which thou knewest not, neither did thy fathers know; that he might make thee know that man doth not live by bread only, but by every word that proceedeth out of the mouth of the LORD doth man live (Deut. 8:3).*

Mt. 5:3ff The Beatitudes...*Blessed are.....*

*Blessed is he whose transgression is forgiven, whose sin is covered. Blessed is the man unto whom the LORD imputeth not iniquity, and in whose spirit there is no guile* (Ps. 32:1,2).

*And said unto them, It is written, My house shall be called the house of prayer; but ye have made it a den of thieves* (Mt. 21:13).

*Even them will I bring to my holy mountain, and make them joyful in my house of prayer: their burnt offerings and their sacrifices shall be accepted upon mine altar; for mine house shall be called an house of prayer for all people* (Isa 56:7).

*Then saith Jesus unto them, All ye shall be offended because of me this night: for it is written, I will smite the shepherd, and the sheep of the flock shall be scattered abroad* (Mt. 26:31).

*Awake, O sword, against my shepherd, and against the man that is my fellow, saith the LORD of hosts: smite the shepherd, and the sheep shall be scattered: and I will turn mine hand upon the little ones (Zech. 13:7).*

Some evidences that the Bible is God's Word:

It is significant that the evidence available and perhaps necessary for the establishment of the Bible as God's word is empirical and not necessarily scientific. It may be, too, that some of these are unique and not representative of other writings considered scripture. Each of these is very significant and together they form a formidable barrage of evidence which cannot be ignored. We have considered some of the direct statements made by the Bible and a few made by Jesus Christ who is the best judge of what is scripture. Not only did He quote the Old Testament as Scripture, the New Testament quotes Him as Scripture. The Holy Spirit, who oversaw the writing of the New Testament, reminded the disciples of what Jesus had said to them. The Gospel of John quotes Jesus as saying: *"But the Comforter, which is the Holy Ghost, whom the Father will send in my name, he shall teach you all things, and bring all things to your remembrance, whatsoever I have said unto you."* (Jn. 14:26). Having accepted the veracity of the person and purpose of Jesus Christ we cannot do less to His words. Of the evidence requiring consideration we have:

1.  The profundity of the Bible. The Bible is very deep in the message which it communicates to man. The plight of man and God's plan of salvation presented in the Bible is unparalleled. No other book, whether original or subsequently edited, lays out such a plan threaded throughout its entirety in the way that the Bible does. Not only does it deal with the origin of man's predicament, it correctly presents his present condition and his eventual future. It presents the only alternative to man's dilemma.

2.  The elaborateness of the Bible speaks volumes to its authenticity. The theme, God's plan of salvation, which runs throughout is traced in such detail that it required the entire compendium of the Bible to unravel. The promise is made of a Son who would crush the Serpent's head though His heel would be bruised (Gen. 3:15). It

traces God's singling out a people, a family line and finally a virgin through whom His salvation would come. It follows His earthly life and fulfillment of the bruising of His heel on the cross to the resurrection of His physical body, thus opening up the way for those who would come after. His eventual crowning victory will come when He returns to take unrighteousness from the world (Rev. 19:11-15).

*"For the preaching of the cross is to them that perish foolishness; but unto us which are saved it is the power of God. For it is written, I will destroy the wisdom of the wise, and will bring to nothing the understanding of the prudent. Where is the wise? Where is the scribe? Where is the disputer of this world? Hath not God made foolish the wisdom of this world?"* (I Cor. 1:18-20).

3. The intricacies of the Bible are simply astounding. Note the way the promise of a Savior is presented so early in the history of man and developed throughout succeeding books and generations despite the depth of the corruption and depravity of man. Nothing has been able to hinder or prevent God's plan. Not even the seeming victory of the Evil one at the cross swayed the progress. As a matter of fact, if the perpetrators of that act had known that this was the very means of their undoing, they would not have carried through with their wickedness.

*But we speak the wisdom of God in a mystery, even the hidden wisdom, which God ordained before the world unto our glory: which none of the princes of this world knew: for had they known it, they would not have crucified the Lord of glory* (I Cor. 2:7, 8).

4. The accuracy of the prophetic is profound. One example is the place of the birth of Christ and events surrounding His birth. Despite the fact that Mary and Joseph were in Nazareth up to the last period before His birth, Christ had to be born in Bethlehem and circumstances made it necessary that they be there. Who would have known, too, that Herod would have reacted to the birth of Christ to the extent that He would wipe out every child under the age of two causing great lamentation? Yet the Old Testament prophets correctly predicted these and other attending events.

*But thou, Bethlehem Ephratah, though thou be little among the thousands of Judah, yet out of thee shall he come forth unto me that is to be ruler in Israel; whose goings forth have been from of old, from everlasting* (Micah 5:2).

*When Israel was a child, then I loved him, and called my son out of Egypt* (Hos.11:1).

5. The unbiased representation of the nature and condition of man is unprecedented and unparalleled. A Jew did not presume to write such an unflattering record of the Israelites. They are reputed to have forsaken their God and adulterated themselves till they were cast out of their land. Neither did they think to categorize all men severally and collectively as unrighteous. Only an aggrieved God who has all knowledge and moral perfection could make such declarations of mankind.

*As it is written, there is none righteous, no, not one: there is none that understandeth, there is none that seeketh after God. They are all gone out of the way, they are together become unprofitable; there is none that doeth good, no, not one* (Rom. 3:10-12).

6. The unflattering history of the Jew is testimony that the Jews did not write the Scriptures to favor themselves. God delivered the Jews from slavery in Egypt but it did not take long for them to rebel against the God who had delivered them. There were few instances where Israel served God but in the main their history until their Babylonian captivity was one of idolatry. God continually chided with them for their ungodliness until He removed them from the possession which He had given them. Even in their ungodliness He maintains His covenant with them.

7. The history which pre-existed man is not myth. Only a God who was present and involved could reveal that information. It is no myth and the record is accurate that God created in seven days. Even now the pattern of time which was established then continues. Day and night follow each other; the seven-day-week cycle continues. Seasons continue as ordered.

*And God said, Let there be lights in the firmament of the heaven to divide the day from the night; and let them be for signs, and for seasons, and for days, and years: and let them be for lights in the firmament of the heaven to give light upon the earth: and it was so. And God made two great lights; the greater light to rule the day, and the lesser light to rule the night: he made the stars also. And God set them in the firmament of the heaven to give light upon the earth, and to rule over the day and over the night, and to divide the light from the darkness: and God saw that it was good* (Gen. 1:14-18).

*And I will establish my covenant with you; neither shall all flesh be cut off any more by the waters of a flood; neither shall there any more be a flood to destroy the earth. And God said, This is the token of the covenant which I make between me and you and every living creature that is with you, for perpetual generations: I do set my bow in the cloud, and it shall be for a token of a covenant between me and the earth. And it shall come to pass, when I bring a cloud over the earth, that the bow shall be seen in the cloud: and I will remember my covenant, which is between me and you and every living creature of all flesh; and the waters shall no more become a flood to destroy all flesh. And the bow shall be in the cloud; and I will look upon it, that I may remember the everlasting covenant between God and every living creature of all flesh that is upon the earth. And God said unto Noah, This is the token of the covenant, which I have established between me and all flesh that is upon the earth* (Gen 9:11-17).

8.  The multiplicity of human writers is phenomenal. A compendium composed by about forty writers is remarkable. We have Jews as well as Gentiles who were used. There were the learned as well as the seemingly unlearned. There were kings as well as shepherds. We have had books co-authored by two or more authors but none like the Bible.

9.  The diversity of locations of the human writers also lends its awe to the evidences being considered. What is mind-boggling is that there neither was a script to follow nor were there notes to refer to. Some of the writers were contemporaries but were separated by miles not easily traversed as we can today.

10. The span of time occupied in the writing of the Bible is also noteworthy. These human writers spanned 1600 years yet there is consistency in the theme and message of the Book. Even all of the sub plots that make up the body of the Bible are consistent in their presentation of the God who authored the book.

## The fulfillment of God's word:

God's word is dynamic in its content. The book of Daniel seems to be a springboard for the development of the world both in terms of what has been and what is to come. From Daniel's perspective it was all future but today it is both historical and futuristic. Daniel's message was both panoramic and detailed in some instances. So detailed was it that some critics have thought that his writings were historical at the time of writing instead of predictive. It was humanly impossible for anyone to predict the future with such accuracy as Daniel did. Indeed it was humanly impossible but Daniel wrote under divine inspiration. What is more interesting is that some of what is written in the book of Daniel had the input of one who did not know and did not fear God.

King Nebuchadnezzar, King of Babylon at the time of the captivity of the Jews, is a great contributor to the revealing of the future. It all started with a dream that God gave to him. Nebuchadnezzar dreamed of an image composed of various metals which he realized was very significant. Strangely enough when morning came he knew he had a dream but could not remember it. Because of the impression the dream had made on him he knew that it meant something significant. He tried to recall and sought the assistance of his wise men but to no avail. His threats of death to all the wise men did not change their predicament although it helped in one way. Daniel, too, was sought out for execution together with the other wise men, although he had not been apprised of the problem before. God stepped in again and not only revealed the dream to Daniel but also gave him the interpretation. Nebuchadnezzar's assent to the dream confirmed that Daniel was not presenting a fabrication.

Having established the authenticity of the dream Daniel was now charged with revealing the meaning of the dream. He was able to do that because the author of the dream had also given him the interpretation. Nebuchadnezzar had seen an image of a man whose head was of gold, his chest and arms were of silver, his belly and thighs were of brass, his legs of iron, and his feet of iron and clay. The dream was not a still picture but a video of the final scene. A stone was cut out without hands and struck the image at its feet. That caused the whole image to crumble and become as powder and scattered in the wind. The stone itself became a great mountain and filled the whole earth.

What did all that mean? Daniel revealed that God had communicated to the king the future of the world. Beginning with Nebuchadnezzar who was identified as the head of gold, the succeeding kingdoms who would rule the world were revealed. They were revealed to Nebuchadnezzar as the second and the next and the next without identifying who the individual kingdoms were. That information was later revealed to Daniel in successive visions. A Babylonian, a non-Jew, was instrumental in the revelation of the future.

Again Nebuchadnezzar was used to communicate a very important message to the inhabitants of the earth. In the fourth chapter of Daniel, which from all indications was written by Nebuchadnezzar, God makes it abundantly clear that he controls the course of this world. Often it would seem that God is far removed and not interested or involved in the affairs of man, but careful consideration of His revelation will convince one otherwise. Nebuchadnezzar recounts his personal experience with God which taught him a very important lesson which was not only for him but for mankind.

His experience came firstly in the form of a dream/vision which he sought explanation of and then in a personal experience which none can deny. It happened to him. Furthermore, all of Babylon could testify to that fact because they experienced it with him.

Nebuchadnezzar dreamed of a great tree which flourished and had far reaching influence and importance. But that tree was cut off with only a stump being left in the ground. A ring of iron and brass was placed around the stump and it remained that way for seven years. The order was given that his heart be changed from that of a man to that of a beast for the duration of these seven years also.

Daniel revealed to the king that the vision was of him and for him and for his detractors (Dan. 4:19). Daniel also revealed the dream in its entirety to the king with the proviso: *'till thou know that the most High ruleth in the kingdom of men, and giveth it to whomsoever he will* (Dan. 4:25). Daniel further admonished the king to: ...*break off thy sins by righteousness, and thine iniquities by showing mercy to the poor; if it may be a lengthening of thy tranquillity* (Dan.4:27).

The king acknowledged Daniel's revelation because he remembered his first dream. But his arrogance and pride got the better of him and he succumbed to his boasting a year later. Immediately the fulfillment of the prophecy of the dream came upon him and he became an animal and was driven from among men. Not until the seven years were accomplished and he again acknowledged God was he restored to normalcy and returned to his throne. During the time of his absence from the throne, no one took or even attempted to take over his kingdom. Thus quothed Nebuchadnezzar:

*And at the end of the days I Nebuchadnezzar lifted up mine eyes unto heaven, and mine understanding returned unto me, and I blessed the most High, and I praised and honoured him that liveth for ever, whose dominion is an everlasting dominion, and his kingdom is from generation to generation: and all the inhabitants of the earth are reputed as nothing: and he doeth according to his will in the army of heaven, and among the inhabitants of the earth: and none can stay his hand, or say unto him, What doest thou?* (Dan. 4:34, 35).

The kingdoms which followed the Babylonian empire are the Medo-Persians (the chest and arms of silver), the Greeks (the belly and thighs of brass), and the Romans (the legs of iron). Yet to come is a revived Roman empire amalgamated with weaker and corrupting elements. This is represented by the feet of a mixture of iron and clay. Also to come is the kingdom of God which will be established on the earth. The first four empires ruled exactly as was predicted in Daniel and history bears that out. Because of the exactness of those fulfillments we can reasonably believe that the rest will occur exactly as Daniel predicted.

God's program for Israel was also revealed to Daniel but let it suffice that this account of the prophetic is exemplary of the other prophetic passages. The Bible is God's word and it will come to pass as He has determined.

# CHAPTER FIVE

# DENOMINATIONS, CULTS AND SECTS

Immediately the heading of this chapter launches us into the quagmire of what has happened to the 'faith that was once delivered unto the saints'. One realizes that there are sections and subsections of a once unified faith and that those sectors divide to the extent that there are not only factions but friction among the groupings. Each of the names above suggests a type of grouping that is not sacrosanct of its self but within each is a myriad of sub-groupings that differ in one way or the other. Definitions of themselves do not clarify the differences nor do they ameliorate the misgivings among them. At best these definitions help in giving an understanding of the magnitude of the problems one faces.

One wonders about the proliferation of religious denominations. The reason is simple. The arch enemy is a tactical deceiver. One would not immediately fall for a religion diametrically opposed to one's faith, (although it sometimes happens). One would be more inclined to gravitate to additional "truth" or the elimination of vital "truth" which slowly draws one away from the fundamental position of the original until the end result bears no resemblance to it. There are those who would establish roots along the way advocating a position which is supposedly fundamental thus giving rise to what we today experience as denominations. Another tactic of the enemy in that light is to cloud the reality with a seemingly reasonable question. "Since there are so many variations (especially among Christians) which one is right? Obviously they can't all be right." Strict adherence to the teachings of Christ without the appendages of man and the devil leaves one with the 'right'.

One understands that there are numerous religions but this chapter deals with the Christian faith as the religion of special consideration. Denominations, cults and sects are dealt with under the umbrella of Christianity for it is this religion we contend for and hope to present as God's provision for mankind. What immediately separates Christianity from other religions is that one believes, because of its inherent source and the 'Great Commission' to its presenters, that this is what God intended. This is done, too, with the understanding that the differences in some cases were orchestrated by the master deceiver with the expressed purpose of creating enough confusion which would result in disillusionment. Such disillusionment would also result in some not wanting any part in organized religion simply because of the diversity. The result is atheism and agnosticism.

**Denomination:**

This is one of the major groupings within Christianity. Although Christianity faced some factions and differences of opinion very early in its history, under the leadership of the Apostles these were controlled and did not thrive to the extent of spawning denominations. Jesus addressed some of these as they raised their ugly heads even while He was establishing this new faith. The Apostles in turn dealt with problems of varying sorts as evidenced by the content of the epistles. These differences came, not as a result of insufficient truth but rather as Paul describes in Second Corinthians.

> *Therefore seeing we have this ministry, as we have received mercy, we faint not; but have renounced the hidden things of dishonesty, not walking in craftiness, nor handling the word of God deceitfully; but by manifestation of the truth commending ourselves to every man's conscience in the sight of God.*
>
> *But if our gospel be hid, it is hid to them that are lost: in whom the god of this world hath blinded the minds of them which believe not, lest the light of the glorious gospel of Christ, who is the image of God, should shine unto them.*
>
> *For we preach not ourselves, but Christ Jesus the Lord; and ourselves your servants for Jesus' sake* (II Cor. 4:1-5).

He further elucidates the problem later in the book when he says:

> *For such are false apostles, deceitful workers, transforming themselves into the apostles of Christ. And no marvel; for Satan himself is transformed into an angel of light. Therefore it is no great thing if his ministers also be transformed as the ministers of righteousness; whose end shall be according to their works* (II Cor. 11:13 – 15).

It becomes immediately obvious that the author of variance is the arch enemy Satan. But are all denominations false? We must very early answer with an unequivocal No! What then is the problem? Don't God and Satan seem to be on the same side? No!

They are not. The problem lies in the intent of Satan. God intended unity, (*Neither pray I for these alone, but for them also which shall believe on me through their word; that they all may be one; as thou, Father, art in me, and I in thee, that they also may be one in us: that the world may believe that thou hast sent me* (Jn. 17:20, 21); but Satan's diversity is meant to confuse. Although different denomination teach basically the same thing, the mere fact that they carry different captions allow for the question, "Why?" Enough doubt is created to cause the confusion.

## But what is a denomination and what are its origins?

Although the tendency was there from early, it was not until the time of the reformation that there was the beginning of the proliferation that we have today. The Church, from the time of Constantine in the early fourth century, began degenerating from what persisted. Persecution under the previous Roman Emperors had steeled the resolve of the early Christians. Constantine changed the atmosphere and granted religious tolerance to Christianity which gave reprieve from persecution but resulted in the compromised quality of believers. The Roman Catholic Church spawned out of what used to be the genuine Christian religion. The slide downward was steady and continuous with theologians crying out periodically against the degeneration. It was not until the time of Martin Luther (a Roman Catholic priest and professor) in the early sixteenth century that there was a major revolt against the Roman Catholic's abuse of Christianity. Then he listed ninety-five doctrinal errors of the Roman Catholic Church with regard to indulgences which he nailed to the door of the church in Wittenberg. That riled up the Church which demanded that he recant. His refusal led to his excommunication and subsequent establishing of what he believed to be what the Bible taught. There was a swell in persons leaving the Roman Catholic Church and a new movement was formed. The movement was called the Reformation. Those who broke away were referred to as Protestants.

## This is how answers.com defines denominations:

"A large group of religious congregations united under a common faith and name and organized under a single administrative and legal hierarchy."[31]

## The phenomenon was further described as such:

"The rise of denominations within the Christian faith can be traced back to the Protestant Reformation, the movement to "reform" the Roman Catholic Church during the 16th century, out of which four major divisions or traditions of Protestantism would emerge: Lutheran, Reformed, Anabaptist, and Anglican. From these four, other denominations grew over the centuries."[32]

The reasons for the differences among denominations are also noteworthy. They were cosmetic and not matters which departed significantly from the basic doctrines of Christianity. They were sometimes simply liturgical.

"The Lutheran denomination was named after Martin Luther and was based on his teachings. The Methodists got their name because their founder, John Wesley, was famous for coming up with "methods" for spiritual growth. Presbyterians are named for their view on church leadership—the Greek word for elder is presbyteros. Baptists got their name because they have always emphasized the importance of baptism. Each denomination has a slightly different doctrine or emphasis from the others, such as the method of baptism; the availability of the Lord's Supper to all or just to those whose testimonies can be verified by church leaders; the sovereignty of God versus free will in the matter of salvation; the future of Israel and the church; pre-tribulation versus post-tribulation rapture; the existence of the "sign" gifts in the modern era, and so on. The point of these divisions is never Christ as Lord and Savior, but rather honest differences of opinion by godly, albeit flawed, people seeking to honor God and retain doctrinal purity according to their consciences and their understanding of His Word."[33]

## Cults:

A Cult is more interesting and much more involved than denomination because of the implications of the name. It must be noted also that these spring up within and around denominations. In some spheres the word 'cult' could be so charged that it would be considered aggressive and antagonistic to even use it. Today there are politically correct terms which would make one's disposition to a cult more palatable or non-offensive. Whatever your persuasion, Christ calls His followers to militancy but not violence.

*The disciple is not above his master, nor the servant above his lord. It is enough for the disciple that he be as his master, and the servant as his lord. If they have called the master of the house Beelzebub, how much more shall they call them of his household?*

*Fear them not therefore: for there is nothing covered, that shall not be revealed; and hid, that shall not be known. What I tell you in darkness, that speak ye in light: and what ye hear in the ear, that preach ye upon the housetops.*

*And fear not them which kill the body, but are not able to kill the soul: but rather fear him which is able to destroy both soul and body in hell. Are not two sparrows sold for a farthing? And one of them shall not fall on the ground without your Father. But the very hairs of your head are all numbered. Fear ye not therefore, ye are of more value than many sparrows.*

*Whosoever therefore shall confess me before men, him will I confess also before my Father which is in heaven. But whosoever shall deny me before men, him will I also deny before my Father which is in heaven.*

*Think not that I am come to send peace on earth: I came not to send peace, but a sword. For I am come to set a man at variance against his father, and the daughter against her mother, and the daughter in law against her mother in law. And a man's foes shall be they of his own household.*

*He that loveth father or mother more than me is not worthy of me: and he that loveth son or daughter more than me is not worthy of me. And he that taketh not his cross, and followeth after me, is not worthy of me. He that findeth his life shall lose it: and he that loseth his life for my sake shall find it. He that receiveth you receiveth me, and he that receiveth me receiveth him that sent me* (Mt. 10:24 – 40).

There may be as wide a variety of definitions of 'cult' as there are persons wishing to be heard on the matter. In each instance there may be a shade of meaning which is unique to the definition. We will list some of those which seem most significant although we will not particularly point out their characteristics.

A cult might also be defined as a group of people gathered about a specific person or person's misinterpretation of the Bible. "...From a theological viewpoint, the cults contain many major deviations from historic Christianity. Yet, paradoxically, they continue to insist that they are entitled to be classified as Christians."[34]

## Martin continues to say:

"Within the theological structure of the cults there is considerable truth, all of which, it might be added, is drawn from Biblical sources, but so diluted with human error as to be more deadly than complete falsehood."[35]

A large group of religious congregations united under a common faith and name and organized under a single administrative and legal hierarchy.[36]

Some dictionaries define 'cult' as:

6. a religious sect considered to be false, unorthodox, or extremist, with members often living outside of conventional society under the direction of a charismatic leader.
7. the members of such a religion or sect
8. any system for treating human sickness that originated by a person usually claiming to have sole insight into the nature of disease, and that employs methods regarded as unorthodox or unscientific.[37]

(Only the last three from this source were selected as the other definitions have reference to non-religious activity.)

## What is a cult?

Sometimes it seems that question has as many answers as there are, well, cults. Yet the term 'cult' has a precise definition – or rather several precise definitions. Which definition is the right one largely depends on the context in which the term 'cult' is applied.[38]

The definition of the term 'cult' as provided by the Merriam-Webster dictionary covers a variety meanings:

1: formal religious veneration : worship
2: a system of religious beliefs and ritual; also: its body of adherents

3: a religion regarded as unorthodox or spurious; also : its body of adherents.[39]

## Cult: Meanings Vary

The term is confusing because it is ambiguous – infused with a variety of meanings depending on who uses it – and for which purpose it is used.

For example, the term 'cult' can be used in a *theological* and/or a *sociological* sense. The word takes on different meanings depending on the context in which it is used.

For instance, a Christian theologian can state that, say, the Mormon Church is theologically a cult of Christianity.

From that perspective – the viewpoint of a Christian – that is true since the Mormon Church rejects, changes or adds to the essential doctrines of the Christian faith to such an extent that Mormonism must be regarded as having separated itself from the faith it claims to represent. While the 'Church of Jesus Christ of Latter-day Saints' claims to be not only Christian in nature but also the only true expression of historical Christianity, Mormonism in reality has usurped and plagiarized Christian terminology and scriptures, creating a new religion.

In other words, the Mormon Church is not a Christian denomination, nor is it a sect – a term often used to indicate a group or movement that, while still part of the faith it identifies with, has doctrines or practices not in line with those of historical Christianity, but usually not to such an extent that it must be considered a different religion altogether. From a Christian perspective that religion fits meaning #2 in the dictionary definition quoted above, since it is a "religion regarded as unorthodox or spurious."[40]

Questions.org carries this unique mainstream definition which must be considered:

## Question: What is the definition of a Cult?

**Answer:** ...The specific Christian definition of a cult is "a religious group that denies one or more of the fundamentals of biblical truth." In simpler terms, a cult is a group that teaches something that will cause a person to remain unsaved if he/she believes it. As distinct from a religion, a cult is a group that claims to be part of the religion, yet denies essential truth(s) of that religion. A Christian cult is a group that denies one or more of the fundamental truths of Christianity, while still claiming to be Christian.

The two most common teachings of cults are that Jesus was not God and that salvation is not by faith alone. A denial of the deity of Christ results in Jesus' death not being a sufficient payment for our sins. A denial of salvation by faith alone results in salvation being achieved by our own works, something the Bible vehemently and consistently denies.[41]

As has been noted before, there are some negative connotations which sometimes accompany the use of the word. These are not inherent in but reflective of the predisposition of particular groupings. As has been mentioned and will be considered in greater detail later, falsehoods and their proponents are not something new. Christ had to contend with them. Their proliferation today should come as no surprise but should be resisted just as stoutly today as Christ and the Apostles did then.

Here are a few of the negative meanings which sometimes accompany the use of the word cult:

### Negative meanings:

- **Evangelical Christians and Counter-Cult Movement (CCM) usage:** They define a cult as any religious group which accepts most but not all of the key historical Christian doctrines (e.g. The divinity of Jesus, Virgin birth, the Trinity, salvation by faith not works, etc.). The implication is that the Cult's theology is invalid; they teach heresy.

- **Fundamentalist Christian usage:** Some fundamentalist would accept the Evangelical definition of cult defined above. Others brand any religious group which deviates from historical Protestant Christian beliefs as a cult.
- **Anti-cult movement** usage: The anti-cult movement (ACM) attempts to raise public consciousness about what they see as dangerous and authoritarian mind control cults and doomsday cults. Most do not care about the faith group's theology. They target only what they see as deceptive practices, and dangerous psychological pressure techniques, such as brainwashing.

**Very negative meaning:**

- **Popular, media usage:** A cult is considered a small, evil religious group, often with a single charismatic leader, that engages in brainwashing and other mind control techniques, believes that the end of the world is imminent, and collects large amounts of weaponry in preparation for a massive war.[42]

**Biblical Recognition:**

The Bible recognizes teachings around the Christian religion which are not consistent with the teachings of Christ. To contend against them is to be consistent with the teachings and practices of Christ. The constant references to persons as false prophets or their teachings as false should be a reminder to Christians to remain vigilant against the incursion of corrupting elements. The following scriptures bear out the claim that the Bible warns against false doctrine. Various forms are even mentioned to show the reality of the factions.

## Doctrines of Men:

> *Let no man beguile you of your reward in a voluntary humility and worshipping of angels, intruding into those things which he hath not seen, vainly puffed up by his fleshly mind, and not holding the Head, from which all the body by joints and bands having nourishment ministered, and knit together, increaseth with the increase of God. Wherefore if ye be dead with Christ from the rudiments of the world, why, as though living in the world, are ye subject to ordinances, (Touch not; taste not; handle not; which all are to perish with the using;) <u>after the commandments and doctrines of men</u>?* (Col. 2:18 – 22).

## Doctrines of devils:

> *Now the Spirit speaketh expressly, that in the latter times some shall depart from the faith, giving heed to <u>seducing spirits, and doctrines of devils</u>; speaking lies in hypocrisy; having their conscience seared with a hot iron; forbidding to marry, and commanding to abstain from meats, which God hath created to be received with thanksgiving of them which believe and know the truth. For every creature of God is good, and nothing to be refused, if it be received with thanksgiving: for it is sanctified by the word of God and prayer* (I Tim. 4:1 - 4).

## Doctrines of Pharisees and Sadducees:

The doctrines of the Pharisees and Sadducees were many and very dangerous. Jesus spoke against them more than any other false doctrine. The constant dissention between Jesus and those groups substantiates the magnitude of the problem they presented. Much is said by Jesus in terms of warning against them and also in identifying some of the areas in which their teachings were false and they were hypocritical.

> *Then Jesus said unto them, Take heed and beware of the <u>leaven of the Pharisees and of the Sadducees.</u>*
>
> *How is it that ye do not understand that I spake it not to you concerning bread, that ye should beware of the leaven of the Pharisees and of the Sadducees?*
>
> *Then understood they how that he bade them not beware of the leaven of bread, but of <u>the doctrine of the Pharisees and of the Sadducees</u>.* (Mt. 16:6, 11-12).

> *The same day came to him the Sadducees, which say that <u>there is no resurrection</u>, and asked him (Mt. 22:23).*

> *Master, which is the great commandment in <u>the law</u>?* (Mt. 22:36).

> *For I say unto you, That except your righteousness shall exceed <u>the righteousness of the scribes and Pharisees,</u> ye shall in no case enter into the kingdom of heaven* (Mt. 5:20).

> *And when the Pharisees saw it, they said unto his disciples, <u>Why eateth your Master with publicans and sinners?</u>* (Mt. 9:11).

*And when the devil was cast out, the dumb spake: and the multitudes marvelled, saying, It was never so seen in Israel. <u>But the Pharisees said, He casteth out devils through the prince of the devils</u>* (Mt. 9:33, 34).

*But when the Pharisees saw it, they said unto him, Behold, thy disciples do <u>that which is not lawful to do upon the Sabbath day</u>* (Mt. 12:2).

*But when the Pharisees heard it, they said, <u>This fellow doth not cast out devils, but by Beelzebub the prince of the devils.</u>*
*But I say unto you, That <u>every idle word</u> that men shall speak, they shall give account thereof in the day of judgment. For by thy words thou shalt be justified, and by thy words thou shalt be condemned. Then certain of the scribes and of the Pharisees answered, saying, Master, <u>we would see a sign from thee</u>* (Mt. 12:24, 36 – 38).

*The Pharisees also came unto him, <u>tempting him</u>, and saying unto him, Is it lawful for a man to put away his wife for every cause?* (Mt. 19:3).

*But <u>the Pharisees and lawyers rejected the counsel of God</u> against themselves, being not baptized of him* (Lk. 7:30).

*In the mean time, when there were gathered together an innumerable multitude of people, insomuch that they trade one upon another, he began to say unto his disciples first of all, Beware ye of <u>the leaven of the Pharisees, which is hypocrisy</u>* (Lk. 12:1).

*The Pharisee stood and prayed thus with himself,
God, I thank thee, that I am not as other men
are, extortioners, unjust, adulterers, or even as this
publican. I fast twice in the week; I give tithes of all
that I possess* (Lk. 18:11, 12).

*Therefore said some of the Pharisees, <u>This man is not of
God, because he keepeth not the Sabbath day.</u> Others
said, How can <u>a man that is a sinner</u> do such miracles?
And there was a division among them* (Jn. 9:16).

*Then many of the Jews which came to Mary, and had
seen the things which Jesus did, believed on him.
    But some of them went their ways to the Pharisees,
and told them what things Jesus had done.
    Then <u>gathered the chief priests and the Pharisees
a council,</u> and said, What do we? For this man doeth
many miracles* (Jn. 11:45 – 47).

*There came also a multitude out of the cities round
about unto Jerusalem, bringing sick folks, and them
which were vexed with unclean spirits: and they were
healed every one. Then the high priest rose up, and
all they that were with him, (which is <u>the sect of the
Sadducees,)</u> and were filled with indignation, and
<u>laid their hands on the apostles, and put them in the
common prison</u>* (Acts 5:16 – 18).

*But when Paul perceived that the one part were
Sadducees, and the other Pharisees, he cried out in
the council, Men and brethren, I am a Pharisee, the
son of a Pharisee: of <u>the hope and resurrection of the
dead</u> I am called in question.*

*And when he had so said, there arose a dissension between the Pharisees and the Sadducees: and the multitude was divided. For the <u>Sadducees say that there is no resurrection, neither angel, nor spirit</u>: but the Pharisees confess both* (Acts23:6 – 8). (underline mine)

## Doctrine of Balaam:

*But I have a few things against thee, because thou hast there them that hold the doctrine of Balaam, who taught Balac <u>to cast a stumbling block before the children of Israel, to eat things sacrificed unto idols, and to commit fornication</u>* (Rev. 2:14). (underline mine)

(Balaam caused Israel to engage in activities contrary to the commands of their God. Even so today there are those who teach things that God did not teach and even things that are contrary to what God has taught. In all this they do it for a price.)

## Doctrine of the Nicolaitanes:

*But this thou hast, that thou hatest <u>the deeds of the Nicolaitanes</u>, which I also hate. (Rev. 2:6)*

*So hast thou also them that hold the <u>doctrine of the Nicolaitanes</u>, which thing I hate (Rev. 2:15). (underline mine)*

(Like Balaam, one Nicholas, encouraged Christians to be licentious and promiscuous and commit sins contrary to Christian doctrine. Peter seemed to be referring to those in II Pet. 2:19, 20).

## Doctrines of Christ:

Christ did not only warn against false doctrines, He also taught the things which mattered to the Kingdom of God. One of his famous teaching sessions is recorded in the Gospels as the 'Sermon on the Mount'. Matthew occupies three chapters recounting that teaching session. He begins chapter five with: *"And seeing the multitudes, he went up into a mountain: and when he was set, his disciples came unto him: and he opened his mouth, and taught them, saying..."* (Matt. 5:1, 2). The lecture ends in chapter seven with these words: *"And it came to pass, when Jesus had ended these sayings, the people were astonished <u>at his doctrine</u>: for he taught them as one having authority, and not as the scribes"* (Matt. 7:28, 29). Jesus established His authority in His teachings, not as one presenting textbook information, but as one presenting authentic revelation.

The Apostles, in presenting those teachings, recognized them as such and presented them with the same fervency.

> *And when they had set them in the midst, they asked, By what power, or <u>by what name</u>, have ye done this?*
>
> *Be it known unto you all, and to all the people of Israel, that <u>by the name of Jesus Christ of Nazareth,</u> whom ye crucified, whom God raised from the dead, even by him doth this man stand here before you whole.*
>
> *Neither is there salvation in any other: <u>for there is none other name under heaven given among men, whereby we must be saved.</u>*
>
> *And they called them, and <u>commanded them not to speak at all nor teach in the name of Jesus.</u> But Peter and John answered and said unto them, Whether it be right in the sight of God to hearken unto you more than unto God, judge ye. For we*

*cannot but speak the things which we have seen and heard* (Acts 4:4, 10, 12, 18 – 20).

*Young men likewise exhort to be sober minded. In all things showing thyself a pattern of good works: in doctrine showing uncorruptness, gravity, sincerity, sound speech, that cannot be condemned; that he that is of the contrary part may be ashamed, having no evil thing to say of you.*

*Exhort servants to be obedient unto their own masters, and to please them well in all things; not answering again; not purloining, but showing all good fidelity; that they may adorn the doctrine of God our Saviour in all things.*

*For the grace of God that bringeth salvation hath appeared to all men, Teaching us that, denying ungodliness and worldly lusts, we should live soberly, righteously, and godly, in this present world; looking for that blessed hope, and the glorious appearing of the great God and our Saviour Jesus Christ; who gave himself for us, that he might redeem us from all iniquity, and purify unto himself a peculiar people, zealous of good works* (Tit. 2:6 – 13).

*Therefore leaving the principles of the doctrine of Christ, let us go on unto perfection; not laying again the foundation of repentance from dead works, and of faith toward God, of the doctrine of baptisms, and of laying on of hands, and of resurrection of the dead, and of eternal judgment* (Heb. 6:1 – 2).

*For many deceivers are entered into the world, who confess not that Jesus Christ is come in the flesh. This is a deceiver and an antichrist* (II Jn. 1:7).

*Whosoever transgresseth, and abideth not in the <u>doctrine of Christ</u>, hath not God. He that abideth in the <u>doctrine of Christ</u>, he hath both the Father and the Son.*

*If there come any unto you, and bring not <u>this doctrine</u>, receive him not into your house, neither bid him God speed: for he that biddeth him God speed is <u>partaker of his evil deeds</u>* (II Jn. 1:9 – 11)

*Now these things were our examples, to the intent <u>we should not lust after evil things</u>, as they also lusted. <u>Neither be ye idolaters</u>, as were some of them; as it is written, The people sat down to eat and drink, and rose up to play.*

*<u>Neither let us commit fornication</u>, as some of them committed, and fell in one day three and twenty thousand.*

*<u>Neither let us tempt Christ</u>, as some of them also tempted, and were destroyed of serpents.*

*<u>Neither murmur ye</u>, as some of them also murmured, and were destroyed of the destroyer.*

*<u>Now all these things happened unto them for ensamples: and they are written for our admonition</u>, upon whom the ends of the world are come.* (I Cor. 10:6 – 11)

*And turning the cities of Sodom and Gomorrha into ashes <u>condemned them</u> with an overthrow, <u>making them an ensample</u> unto those that after should live ungodly;* (II Pet. 2:6). (underline mine)

Nothing delineates more between Christianity and Judaism than the command that Christ gave to his disciples: *"beware of the doctrines of the Pharisees and the Sadducees"*

Mt. 16:12. In Rom. 7:1-4 one must be dead to the Law in order to be married to Christ. Even the house of Christ is presented as separate from the house of Moses. The house of Christ is Christianity, and the house of Moses is the keeping of The Law. Christianity and the keeping of the Law are incompatible.

*For every house is builded by some man; but he that built all things is God.*

*And Moses verily was faithful in all his house, as a servant, for a testimony of those things which were to be spoken after; but Christ as a son over his own house; whose house are we, if we hold fast the confidence and the rejoicing of the hope firm unto the end.*

*For we are made partakers of Christ, if we hold the beginning of our confidence stedfast unto the end;* (Heb. 3:4 – 6, 14).

*Know ye not, brethren, (for I speak to them that know the law,) how that the law hath dominion over a man as long as he liveth? For the woman which hath an husband is bound by the law to her husband so long as he liveth; but if the husband be dead, she is loosed from the law of her husband. So then if, while her husband liveth, she be married to another man, she shall be called an adulteress: but if her husband be dead, she is free from that law; so that she is no adulteress, though she be married to another man.*

*Wherefore, my brethren, ye also are become dead to the law by the body of Christ; that ye should be married to another, even to him who is raised from the dead, that we should bring forth fruit unto God* (Rom. 7:1 – 4).

Christianity is a new entity born since the resurrection of Christ and not an adjunct of Judaism. Judaism is based in the Old Testament stemming from the deliverance of the Children of Israel from Egypt until Christ. Christianity starts with Christ. Judaism concerns itself with the Old Testament while Christianity embraces the whole Bible. The scripture the Christians embrace is for:

> *All scripture is given by inspiration of God, and <u>is profitable for doctrine, for reproof, for correction, for instruction in righteousness</u>: that the man of God may be perfect, thoroughly furnished unto all good works* (II Tim. 3:16, 17) (underline mine)

The Bible is not all doctrine but all of the Bible is profitable.

## Marks of a cult:

We have seen from the scripture passages quoted that cults are a reality that the Church must contend with. These cults vary depending on what their error is and to what extent they have taken their teachings. In some instances their faults are doctrinally based whereas in others it is the leader who has usurped a position to which he is not entitled. In the case of the Pharisees and Sadducees we saw them wrongfully accusing Jesus of serving the devil as opposed to their own actions. It is a reality that some people are serving the Devil, but who are they? Care must be taken not to make wrong accusations because one may well find himself speaking against the work of God. Jesus Christ warned against speaking against the work of God through the Holy Spirit. False accusations against Him could be forgiven, but there is no forgiveness for the one who blasphemes the Holy Spirit.

Another eye-opener is the dreadful comments made by Jesus Christ about some who may seem to be working for Him. It is obvious that hypocrisy and counterfeit will be present in the promotion of the Kingdom of God. But God's word is constant and it can be correctly applied which would leave those which are contrary in error.

*Wherefore by their fruits ye shall know them.*

*Not every one that saith unto me, Lord, Lord, shall enter into the kingdom of heaven; but he that doeth the will of my Father which is in heaven. Many will say to me in that day, Lord, Lord, have we not prophesied in thy name? And in thy name have cast out devils? And in thy name done many wonderful works?*

*And then will I profess unto them, I never knew you: depart from me, ye that work iniquity* (Matt. 7:20 -23).

It is necessary, therefore, to know the truth.

Dr. Dave Breeze, in his book "Know the Marks of Cults", lists in his chapter headings some of the marks as such:

1. Extra Biblical revelation. ( Heb.1:1; Jn. 8:31)
2. A false basis of Salvation (Tit. 3:5; Rom. 3:23 -26, 28; 4:4, 5; 5:1)
3. An uncertain hope (You are sealed Eph. 1:13; II Cor. 5:1; Phil 1:23; 3:20-21; Col. 1:13; 3:4; I Thess. 4:17; II Tim. 1:8 - 10; I Cor.15:19)
4. Presumptuous Messianic Leadership (I Tim. 2:5; Matt. 23:8-12; Heb. 4:14-16)
5. Doctrinal ambiguity - (II Tim. 3:1 – 10; 1 Jn. 5:11 – 15; I Jn. 2:18 – 29)

6. The claim of special discoveries – (Discoveries of new revelations - Jn.5:31, 39; 10:25; II Pet. 1:19 – 21; 1:16)
7. Defective Christology –
   a. The Deity of Christ Col 2:8 – 10; Jn. 5:23;
   b. The Humanity of Christ Jn. 1:1 – 3, 14; I Jn. 4:2, 3.
8. Segmented Biblical attention
9. Enslaving organizational structure
10. Financial exploitation
11. Denunciation of others
12. Syncretism – (becoming all things to all men. Incorporating all in one. Ecumenism.) (Scripture references supplied)

## Sects:

'Sects' is another word used to describe small breakaway groupings. It is an interesting word because it is sometimes used interchangeably with the word cult. It is further interesting because it is used in the Bible. As will be seen, it is used seemingly as a modern day term for breakaway groups but its Biblical use and definition will show that it may be just as old as Christianity.

One source, Wikipedia, offers this as the definition of sect:

From Wikipedia, the free encyclopedia

A **sect** is a group with distinctive religious, political or philosophical beliefs. Although in past it was mostly used to refer to religious groups, it has since expanded and in modern culture can refer to any organization that breaks away from a larger one to follow a different set of rules and principles.[43]

Following the definition is the etymology of the word:

## Etymology of the word "sect"

The word *sect* comes from the Latin noun *secta* (a feminine form of a variant past participle of the verb *sequi*, to follow), meaning "(beaten) path", and figuratively a (prescribed) way, mode, or manner, and hence metonymously, a discipline or school of thought as defined by a set of methods and doctrines. The present gamut of meanings of *sect* has been influenced by confusion with the homonymous (but etymologically unrelated) Latin word *secta* (the feminine form of the past participle of the verb *secare*, to cut), as sects were scissions cut away from the mainstream religion. Note that speakers of some other languages use the same word for both the meaning *sect* and the meaning *cult*, for example in Italian: *seta*.[44]

Another offering for the meaning and use of the word "sect" is what we find below:

## Meaning of the word *"sect"*

"A sect is a small religious group that is an offshoot of an established religion or denomination. It holds most beliefs in common with its religion of origin, but has a number of novel concepts which differentiate them from that religion. However, in many countries, the term *"sect"* takes on the negative meanings associated with the word *"cult"*. The two terms are considered synonyms in some cases.

Many religions started as sects. One well-known example was the Nazarenes. This was an reform movement within Judaism formed by Jesus' apostles after the execution of Jesus circa 30 CE. They were largely dispersed or killed some four decades later when the Romans attacked Jerusalem and destroyed the temple."[45]

The word 'sect' is not as recent as one may think but goes back even to Bible times. It is a word which has not changed much if any. The major change may be only in sentiments expressed with the usage.

## In Bible times it meant:

Act of choosing, party [46]

Thayer's Greek-English Lexicon renders the meaning thus:

αἵρεσις- airesis

1. Act of taking, capture
2. Choosing, choice
3. That which is chosen, a chosen course of thought and action; hence ones chosen opinion, tenet; according to the context, an opinion varying from the true exposition of the Christian faith (heresy) II Pet. 2:1
4. A body of men separating themselves from others and following their own tenets [a sect, or party]: as the Sadducees (Acts 5:17; the Pharisees (Acts 15:5; 26:5; the Christians, Acts 24:5, 14 (in both instances with a suggestion of reproach); in other writings - used of the schools of philosophy.
5. Dissensions arising from diversity of opinions and aims: Gal.5:20; I Cor. 11:19. [47]

The word, as used in the Bible, seems to carry the same connotation as it does today. It carries with it the same sting thought to be ill-tempered and unacceptable today. The word was used of the strictest sub-grouping of Judaism who considered themselves the elite of their religion. It was used, too, of a second sub-grouping who also held prestigious position. What is remarkable is that as convenience dictated they peacefully co-existed.

Luke, in his Gospel, gives the five usages of the word found in the Bible. By way of explanation, he names one of the groups referred to as a sect: *"Then the high priest rose up, and all they that were with him, (which is* **the sect of the Sadducees,***) and were filled with indignation, "* (Acts 5:17). Again Luke uses it of the most prestigious of the Jewish religion: *"But there rose up certain of the* **sect of the Pharisees** *which believed, saying, That it was needful to circumcise them, and to command them to keep the law of Moses"* (Acts 15:5).

Paul uses the word once of the group to which he at one time so proudly belonged: *"Which knew me from the beginning, if they would testify, that after the* **most straitest sect of our religion I lived a Pharisee"** (Acts 26:5).

Once, the Pharisees, Paul's accusers, used the word with reference to the followers of Christ. It can well be understood that they would opt to refer to Christianity in this way considering their antagonism to Christ.

Paul had been accused of atrocities against the Jews and was mobbed when Claudius Lysias, the Chief Captain of the division of the Roman Army in Jerusalem, rescued him and sent him to Caesarea to stand trial before the Roman Governor, Felix. At the trial, Tertullus, the spokesman for the High Priest, in his opening remarks, refers to the Christian faith as a sect. He is quoted by Luke as saying: *"For we have found this man a pestilent fellow, and a mover of sedition among all the Jews throughout the world, and a ringleader of the* **sect of the Nazarenes"** (Acts 24:5). From all indications, this was one of the ways in which Christianity was castigated for he expected the governor to understand.

Paul had to stand in his defense before the Roman authorities because he had appealed to Caesar. His previous trial seemed on the way to being botched and Paul would not allow that to happen. In order to get a fairer trial as a Roman citizen, he had desired his case to be heard at the highest court. The case briefings had not reached Rome yet but the authorities would hear of Paul what the problem was. In their pre-trial interrogation they made this comment to Paul: *"But we desire to hear of thee what thou thinkest:* ***for as concerning this sect****, we know that every where it is spoken against"* (Acts 28:22).

## Sectarianism - a heresy:

In four other passages in the New Testament, the word translated "sect" in the preceding passages is translated "heresy". No apology is made neither for the use of the word nor for the connotation in which it is used. Whatever it represented was false and stoutly opposed by the founding fathers – the Apostles.

In Acts twenty-four Paul correctly uses the derogatory term by which his faith was castigated by its opposition. Paul made no apology that they were called that neither did he take offence, but went on to affirm that this was where his faith lay. He expressed unequivocal approval for, acceptance of, faith in and hope through the tenets of that "sect". Paul touts this as the way to gain and keep God's approval.

> *But this I confess unto thee, that after the way which they call* <u>heresy</u>*, so worship I the God of my fathers, believing all things which are written in the law and in the prophets: and have hope toward God, which they themselves also allow, that there shall be a resurrection of the dead, both of the just and unjust. And herein do I exercise myself, to have always a conscience void of offence toward God, and toward men* (Acts 24:14).

Paul uses the term again when he chides the Corinthians regarding their behavior in their church services. He was not commending them but was laying it heavily on them that they had behaved in such an ungodly (non-Christian) manner. He goes on to present the alternative to their present behavior in the rest of the chapter following our quote.

> *For first of all, when ye come together in the church, I hear that there be divisions among you; and I partly believe it. For there must be also <u>heresies</u> among you, that they which are approved may be made manifest among you* (I Cor. 11:18, 19).

The Galatians were faulted for having departed from the teachings they had received from Paul. Not only were they reprimanded for their short comings but were offered a list of some of the things of which God disapproves. They are called the 'works of the flesh'. Among the listing is the sin of heresy. Can one countenance a 'heretical sect' (pardon the redundancy) when it is listed among some of the most heinous sins?

> *Now the works of the flesh are manifest, which are these; Adultery, fornication, uncleanness, lasciviousness, idolatry, witchcraft, hatred, variance, emulations, wrath, strife, seditions, heresies, envyings, murders, drunkenness, revellings, and such like: of the which I tell you before, as I have also told you in time past, that they which do such things shall not inherit the kingdom of God.* (Gal. 5:19 – 21)

The Apostle Peter (the one to whom Jesus apparently gave the keys of heaven - Matt. 16:18, 19) lends his voice against false teachers and their teachings. His adjective for their heresies is "damnable". The path that these tread leads to "swift destruction". They are the cause of many of the reproachful remarks leveled at the truth of the Gospel.

> *But there were false prophets also among the people, even as there shall be false teachers among you,*

*who privily shall bring in damnable heresies, even
denying the Lord that bought them, and bring upon
themselves swift destruction. And many shall follow
their pernicious ways; by reason of whom the way of
truth shall be evil spoken of (II Pet. 2:1, 2).*

## Is Christianity a "sect"?

Christianity will be considered briefly under two
perspectives i.e. Christ's declarations regarding what He
had come to do and how the author of Hebrews contrasted
Christianity and Judaism.

Christ left no doubt in the minds of His hearers that
he was not reforming Judaism neither was he perpetuating
its tenets. While Jesus Christ came under Jewish law, His
purpose was to so live and die that He might *"...redeem
them that were under the Law"* (Gal. 4:5). Paul, therefore,
admonishes that Christians should *"Stand fast in the liberty
wherewith Christ has made us free..."* (Gal 5:1). Jesus used
several illustrations to bring home the fact that this was a
new entity. In one instance He informed His hearers that
one cannot put **New Wine** into old bottles lest both the
bottle and the wine perish. This was a direct reference to
their perception of intermingling of His movement with
Judaism.

A second illustration was the use of **cloth**. Jesus
contrasted them thus: *"No man putteth a piece of new cloth
unto an old garment, for that which is put in to fill it up taketh
from the garment, and the rent is made worse"* (Matt. 9:16).
Christianity is not a patch-up of Judaism.

Jesus also informed his hearers that although His work
started small it would result in a massive organism. He said
this:

*Another parable put he forth unto them, saying, The
kingdom of heaven is like to a grain of mustard seed,*

*which a man took, and sowed in his field: which*
*indeed is the least of all seeds: but when it is grown,*
*it is the greatest among herbs, and becometh a tree,*
*so that the birds of the air come and lodge in the*
*branches thereof (Matt. 13:31, 32).*

Jesus claimed that His teachings would be very effective. As leaven (an unusual object to illustrate the kingdom) the progress of the Kingdom would be quiet, unobserved yet dynamic. He states: *"Another parable spake he unto them; The kingdom of heaven is like unto leaven, which a woman took, and hid in three measures of meal, till the whole was leavened"* (Matt. 13:33).

Another claim of Jesus was in conversation with Peter. Peter had just correctly identified who Jesus was. Jesus was the Christ, the Son of the Living God. To that Jesus replied, *"And I say also unto thee, That thou art Peter, and upon this rock I will build my church; and the gates of hell shall not prevail against it"* (Matt. 16:18). Jesus here declared two things concerning the Church which are very significant. 1. I will build my church and 2. The gates of hell shall not prevail against it. It is significant that even at that point in His ministry Christ used the future tense regarding His Church. It was an entity that He would establish and nothing would prevent its establishment and development.

The author of Hebrews has no qualms about the differences between Judaism and Christianity. Though they both have parallels - priestly systems - the orders are different (Heb. 7:1ff). Another major difference in the priesthood is the realm of office. Judaism has an earthly priesthood through the line of Aaron, Christianity has a heavenly High Priest with an unchanging Priesthood after the order of Melchisedec. This discourse is not only to contrast the two systems but also to identify some of the differences as underlined below.

*Now of the things which we have spoken this is the sum: We have such an high priest, who is <u>set on the right hand of the throne of the Majesty in the heavens</u>; a minister of the sanctuary, and <u>of the true tabernacle</u>, which the Lord pitched, and not man.*

*For <u>if he were on earth, he should not be a priest</u>, seeing that there are priests that offer gifts according to the law:*

*But now hath he obtained <u>a more excellent ministry</u>, by how much also <u>he is the mediator of a better covenant</u>, which was <u>established upon better promises</u>. For if that <u>first covenant</u> had been faultless, then should no place have been sought for <u>the second</u>. For finding fault with them, he saith, Behold, the days come, saith the Lord, when I will make <u>a new covenant</u> with the house of Israel and with the house of Judah:*

*In that he saith, A new covenant, <u>he hath made the first old</u>. Now that which decayeth and waxeth <u>old is ready to vanish away</u>* (Heb. 8:1, 2, 4, 6 - 8, 13).

*But Christ being come an high priest of good things to come, by a <u>greater and more perfect tabernacle, not made with hands</u>, that is to say, not of this building; <u>neither by the blood of goats and calves</u>, but <u>by his own blood he entered in once into the holy place, having obtained eternal redemption for us</u>.*

*And for this cause <u>he is the mediator of the new testament</u>, that by means of death, for the <u>redemption of the transgressions that were under the first testament</u>, they which are called might receive the promise of eternal inheritance* (Heb. 9:11, 12, 15). (underline mine)

Denominationalism, Cultism, and Sectarianism, each has its distraction from main line Christianity. Like the

Apostles, one must be aware that all religions are not the same. For this reason one must know the truth about Christianity and not be discomfited in the face of the plethora of others existent today. While one needs to contend for the faith as admonished by Jude, one needs not be disparaging to those who are yet without the truth. Christians are still in the world to bring others to Christ (II Cor. 5:20).

## The study of other religions:

From a Christian perspective, the study of other religions should not be to examine ways to peacefully co-exist but should be an exercise of familiarizing oneself with the tenets of those other religions in order to, in an intellectual way, contend for the doctrines of Christianity. Such familiarization would expose one to the flaws and inaccuracies of false religion in such a way as to pinpoint where these have gone wrong. While such study is not an absolute necessity to present the claims of Christianity it is, nonetheless, a useful tool in contrasting beliefs when engaging others intellectually. It is advantageous to understand the other's perspective in order to redirect his thinking into the right 'way'.

# CHAPTER SIX

# THE CLAIMS OF CHRIST - PART I

**His claim to divinity:**

While it is true that even Jesus said that if one bears witness of himself his witness is not true, yet Jesus' witness of Himself is true because He is "truth" (Jn. 14:6). Jesus claimed to be God. We have seen, too, that Jesus called on other sources to corroborate His claims. He referred to the witness of the Father who testified of Him. He declared His death and resurrection before it happened as authentication of His claims. He asked to accept the report of His works as verification of His authenticity. His conduct among men testified on his behalf. The officers of the Pharisees testified "…'Never man spake like this man,'" (Jn. 7:46). Jesus had more than two witnesses other than Himself to testify of Him. We can and must accept His testimony for it is in keeping with what other Bible characters have said of Him.

Outside the Bible others have attested to the divinity of Christ by recognizing the veracity of the statements made by Christ, the accuracy of the fulfillment of prophecy in the life of Christ, and the probability of that happening in such magnitude whether in the life of Christ or in any other. The probability of one making such prophecies happen in His life is astronomical. Here's Geisler on the matter:

"The word of God will be fulfilled by an act of God. As the writer of the Hebrews states it, *"God also bore witness by signs and wonders and various miracles and by gifts of the Holy spirit…"* (Heb. 2:4). If in the life of Jesus of Nazareth, who claimed fulfillment of these predictions about the Messiah made hundreds of years before, there came to pass all that had been prophesied of him, then we must conclude that he indeed is the Messiah. In short, if Jesus fulfilled the prophecies about the coming Messiah, the fulfillment must be an act of God showing him to be the Son of God."[48]

Geisler proffers that the fulfillment of Old Testament prophecy in the life of Jesus Christ was indeed a miracle. It met all the criteria necessary to authenticate a miracle. He sums up that fact in this way:

"All of the earmarks of a miracle surround Jesus' fulfillment of Old Testament prophecy. (Here he cross references chapter 14 for further definition of a miracle) (1) It was an *unusual event*; the chances were highly improbable; (2) It was accompanied by *theological truth* claims to be the Son of God and the fulfillment of messianic prophecy; (3) The event of Christ's coming brought with it *moral good* through his teaching, life, and influence; (4) The incarnation was not a scientific misfit; it was *supernatural* but not *unnatural*. His miracles not only fit the natural order but they helped the natural order fulfill itself by way of the resurrection. In all these ways the first coming of Christ does indeed qualify as a miracle, that is, as an act of God that confirms the message of God and brings glory to God. And in the case of this particular miracle of the incarnation, it is an act of God that proves Christ to be the unique Son of God. In short, Christ's claims to be God are confirmed by the miracle of the fulfillment of messianic prophecy in His life and death."[49]

At the onset of His ministry, Jesus established the fact that only God must be worshipped. Satan had brazenly offered Jesus, the creator of the universe, to give him the kingdoms of the earth if only He would bow down and worship him (Mt. 4:8 - 10). Jesus knew the meaning of worship and quoted also the written word in His response to Satan. In today's world "your worship" is lightly used to refer to magistrates and judges of the court system. Jesus was under no delusion though He had just fasted for forty days. He was fully cognizant of what it meant to bow down to another, especially in the form that Satan demanded. Only God is deserving of such reverence.

## Jesus accepts worship:

Knowing the principle that only God was to be worshipped is established throughout the Old Testament. One of the great contentions God had with the Children of Israel was regarding worship. They were strictly cautioned that this is one of the things which would cause God to turn around and punish them. But Israel persistently vexed God with their idolatry. God warned them in these words:

> And he said, Behold, I make a covenant: before all thy people I will do marvels, such as have not been done in all the earth, nor in any nation: and all the people among which thou art shall see the work of the LORD: for it is a terrible thing that I will do with thee.
>
> Observe thou that which I command thee this day: behold, I drive out before thee the Amorite, and the Canaanite, and the Hittite, and the Perizzite,

*and the Hivite, and the Jebusite. Take heed to thyself, lest thou make a covenant with the inhabitants of the land whither thou goest, lest it be for a snare in the midst of thee: but ye shall destroy their altars, break their images, and cut down their groves: <u>for thou shalt worship no other god</u>: for the LORD, whose name is Jealous, is a jealous God: lest thou make a covenant with the inhabitants of the land, and they go a whoring after their gods, and do sacrifice unto their gods, and one call thee, and thou eat of his sacrifice; and thou take of their daughters unto thy sons, and their daughters go a whoring after their gods, and make thy sons go a whoring after their god* (Ex. 34:10 – 16).

*Take ye therefore good heed unto yourselves; for ye saw no manner of similitude on the day that the LORD spake unto you in Horeb out of the midst of the fire: lest ye corrupt yourselves, and make you a graven image, the similitude of any figure, the likeness of male or female, the likeness of any beast that is on the earth, the likeness of any winged fowl that flieth in the air, the likeness of any thing that creepeth on the ground, the likeness of any fish that is in the waters beneath the earth: and lest thou lift up thine eyes unto heaven, and when thou seest the sun, and the moon, and the stars, even all the host of heaven, shouldest be driven to worship them, and serve them, which the LORD thy God hath divided unto all nations under the whole heaven* (Deut. 4:15 – 19). (underline mine)

When Solomon erected the Temple unto God and had dedicated it, God covenanted with Him regarding how he and his people could maintain good relations with Him.

That relationship depended on their compliance with God's commands and not worshipping idols as their gods. Israel conceded but soon, even under Solomon, started worshipping idols. These were God's word to Solomon.

> *And the LORD said unto him, I have heard thy prayer and thy supplication, that thou hast made before me: I have hallowed this house, which thou hast built, to put my name there for ever; and mine eyes and mine heart shall be there perpetually.*
>
> *And if thou wilt walk before me, as David thy father walked, in integrity of heart, and in uprightness, to do according to all that I have commanded thee, and wilt keep my statutes and my judgments: then I will establish the throne of thy kingdom upon Israel for ever, as I promised to David thy father, saying, There shall not fail thee a man upon the throne of Israel.*
>
> *But if ye shall at all turn from following me, ye or your children, and will not keep my commandments and my statutes which I have set before you, <u>but go and serve other gods, and worship them</u>; then will I cut off Israel out of the land which I have given them; and this house, which I have hallowed for my name, will I cast out of my sight; and Israel shall be a proverb and a byword among all people:...* (1 Kg. 9:4 – 7).(underline mine).

After Israel had violated their covenant with God and had been exiled and were now back in their own land, the prophet Nehemiah acknowledged God, the only one to be worshipped, thus:

> *Thou, even thou, art LORD alone; thou hast made heaven, the heaven of heavens, with all their host, the*

*earth, and all things that are therein, the seas, and all that is therein, and thou preservest them all; and the host of heaven worshippeth thee* (Neh. 9:6).

Angels did not accept worship:

*And the angel of the LORD said unto Manoah, Though thou detain me, I will not eat of thy bread: and if thou wilt offer a burnt offering, thou must offer it unto the LORD. For Manoah knew not that he was an angel of the LORD* (Jud. 13:16).

In the New Testament we have record of John bowing down before an angel. He had been overwhelmed by the revelation that had been expounded to him that his response was to worship. But the angel did not allow him to do so for the angel knew that only one must be worshipped and that was God. Here is the reaction of the angel:

*And he saith unto me, 'Write, Blessed are they which are called unto the marriage supper of the Lamb.' And he saith unto me, 'These are the true sayings of God.' And I fell at his feet to worship him. And he said unto me, 'See thou do it not: I am thy fellowservant, and of thy brethren that have the testimony of Jesus: worship God: for the testimony of Jesus is the spirit of prophecy'* (Rev. 19:9, 10).

Jesus knew the teachings of the Old Testament, believed in them and kept them. Yet, repeatedly, we see persons paying homage to Jesus and he did not forbid them. He effectively accepted something that belonged only to God. At least nine times, Jesus was worshipped physically and He was aware of it and did not forbid it.

In Matthew, we are told of a leper who came to Jesus for healing. His first action was to worship Christ and call him Lord. Jesus took the leper's greeting and actions in stride as though it were expected and right (Matt. 8:2).

In Matthew 9:18, Christ is teaching when a "certain ruler" came to Him on behalf of his dead daughter. He requests that Jesus come and raise her. Firstly, in his approach, the ruler worshipped as he came to Jesus. Secondly, His request to resurrect his daughter was one where he had faith in Jesus Christ regarding his request. Jesus responded to both incidents positively.

Matthew tells us again that the disciples of Jesus were on the sea experiencing threatening times when Jesus came walking on the water. Jesus has superseded the laws of nature. Peter went out on the water to meet Him and they returned into the boat together. After Jesus got into the boat, the disciples worshipped Him (Matt. 14:33).

A woman from the coast of Tyre and Sidon came to Jesus with the plea that her daughter was possessed with a devil and desired that Jesus heal her. He did not respond the first time but since she persisted He engaged her in conversation. The disciples wanted to send her away but she continued, this time worshipping Him. Jesus then granted her request and healed her daughter (Matt 15:20- 28).

The mother of James and John came to Jesus worshipping as He was informing His disciples concerning His death which was soon to take place. Her desire was that Jesus allow her two sons to sit with Him when He entered into His kingdom. She wanted one on the left and the other on the right. While Jesus did not grant her request He did not reject her worship (Matt. 20:18 – 23).

Jesus had been crucified and laid in a tomb. Because the Sabbath was almost upon them it would seem that the ladies did not do all that they would have liked to prepare the body for burial. Early on the first day of the week, they came to the tomb and found the stone, which had secured it, rolled away. With great consternation, the ladies turned and hurried off to tell the disciples what they thought had happened. As they turned to go, Jesus met them. They grabbed His feet and worshipped. Jesus did not stop them (Matt. 28:9).

The disciples had been commanded to meet Jesus on a mountain in Galilee. They did as they were ordered and met Jesus there. Upon seeing Him, they worshipped Him. Jesus did not prevent them from doing so (Matt. 28:17).

Mark reports one other instance when Jesus was worshipped and did not refuse it. When Jesus came into the country of the Gadarenes, a man who was possessed with devils came out to meet Him. As the man approached the demons cried out because Jesus had commanded them to leave. The man worshipped even while the demons were still in him. Didn't the demons know who Jesus was? They did; yet they, too, worshipped. (Mark 5:6)

John, too, gave another incident which the other writers did not mention. There was a blind man whom Jesus had healed earlier. In His excitement at being able to see, He did not even recognize who had healed Him. He met Jesus again and Jesus asked him, "Do you believe on the Son of God?" The man wanted to know who the Son of God was, because it was his desire to honor Him. Jesus identified himself as the Son of God and the man worshiped Him (Jn. 9:38).

There were other recorded occasions when Jesus was worshipped but it would seem that He could do nothing about those instances. At His birth, Jesus was worshipped. Maybe He was too small to know. (Matt. 2:11) Then at His trial the soldiers mockingly worshipped Him (Mk. 15:19). At His ascension Jesus' disciples worshipped Him as He was taken away from them into heaven (Lk. 24: 52).

Every one of the four Gospels has at least one instance where Jesus was worshipped. But the worship that is most striking is that found in the book of Hebrews. God, Himself, is recorded as saying the words found in Hebrews 1:6. *And again, when he bringeth in the firstbegotten into the world, he saith, 'And let all the angels of God worship him.'* God, who will not share His glory with another, requires the same honor due to Him from the angels for Jesus Christ, His first begotten. If God recognized Jesus as equal with Him, we can do no less.

**Jesus made statements:**

Not only did Jesus claim deity for Himself as He accepted worship of all who recognized His worth, but He made assertions which left no doubt that He claimed deity for Himself. His hearers did not misunderstand His sayings when Jesus used terms which indicated that He thought He was God. In the English language, it may sound like Jesus was being vague or evasive in his actions and responses but to the Jew, Jesus was very plain in his pronouncements. That, the High Priest understood, and therefore accused Him of blasphemy. Having declared His deity in their presence, they dispensed with the need of witnesses. They became judge, jury and witness in their case against Christ.

> *And said, This fellow said, I am able to destroy the temple of God, and to build it in three days.*
> *And the high priest arose, and said unto him, Answerest thou nothing? What is it which these witness against thee?*
> *But Jesus held his peace. And the high priest answered and said unto him, I adjure thee by the living God, that thou tell us whether thou be the Christ, the Son of God. But Jesus held his peace.*
> *Jesus saith unto him, Thou hast said: nevertheless I say unto you, hereafter shall ye see the Son of Man*

*sitting on the right hand of power, and coming in the clouds of heaven.*

*Then the high priest rent his clothes, saying, He hath spoken blasphemy; what further need have we of witnesses? Behold, now ye have heard his blasphemy. What think ye? They answered and said, He is guilty of death* (Mt. 26:61 – 66).

In a previous conversation with the Jews, Jesus was subject to attempted murder by His own countrymen. They pressed for a direct answer regarding His deity as though Christ had not been plain before. To their insistence He responded accordingly. His response infuriated them. They tried to kill Him by stoning Him. Jesus challenged their actions with the question of "Why?" They would not kill Him for His good works, but for blasphemy.

For the second time in the same conversation, the Jews became incensed and tried to mob Jesus. By His speech He had laid claim to His divinity. This time Jesus used His divine power and eluded their onslaught. Though they had not believed His speech, they should have considered His action.

*Then came the Jews round about him, and said unto him, How long dost thou make us to doubt? If thou be the Christ, tell us plainly.*

*Jesus answered them, I told you, and ye believed not: the works that I do in my Father's name, they bear witness of me.*

*But ye believe not, because ye are not of my sheep, as I said unto you. My sheep hear my voice, and I know them, and they follow me: and I give unto them eternal life; and they shall never perish, neither shall any man pluck them out of my hand. My Father, which gave them me, is greater than all;*

*and no man is able to pluck them out of my Father's hand. I and my Father are one.*

*Then the Jews took up stones again to stone him.*

*Jesus answered them, Many good works have I showed you from my Father; for which of those works do ye stone me?*

*The Jews answered him, saying, 'For a <u>good work we stone thee not; but for blasphemy; and because that thou, being a man, makest thyself God</u>'.*

*Jesus answered them, Is it not written in your law, I said, 'Ye are gods?' If he called them gods, unto whom the word of God came, (and the scripture cannot be broken); Say ye of him, whom the Father hath sanctified, and sent into the world, Thou blasphemest; because I said, I am the Son of God?*

*If I do not the works of my Father, believe me not. But if I do, though ye believe not me, believe the works: that ye may know, and believe, that the Father is in me, and I in him.*

*Therefore <u>they sought again to take him</u>: but he escaped out of their hand...*(Jn. 10:24 – 39). (underline mine)

Jesus had had that contention with them before. He had healed a man by the pool of Bethesda, and had ordered him to carry his bed and to go home. The Jews had seen the man doing what they considered to be unlawful on the Sabbath day and had queried. The man did not know who had asked him to do that but was simply overjoyed that he was able to walk and work. The Jews did not share his joy but were more concerned that the man worked on the Sabbath and wanted to know who had caused him to break the Sabbath.

Jesus, too, had worked on the Sabbath although He did no physical work. The fact that he had spoken healing into the life of the crippled man was overbearing. For that reason, they wanted to kill Him.

Jesus compounded the distaste toward Him when he made reference to God as His Father. It was a personalized claim that made Him God also. That the Jews could not countenance. They determined to kill Him for it.

> *Afterward Jesus findeth him in the temple, and said unto him, Behold, thou art made whole: sin no more, lest a worse thing come unto thee.*
>
> *The man departed, and told the Jews that it was Jesus, which had made him whole. And therefore did the Jews persecute Jesus, and sought to slay him, because he had done these things on the Sabbath day.*
>
> *But Jesus answered them, My Father worketh hitherto, and I work.*
>
> *Therefore the Jews sought the more to kill him, because he not only had broken the Sabbath, but said also that God was his Father, making himself equal with God* (Jn. 5:14 – 18). (underline mine)

On one other occasion Jesus demonstrated His divinity and caused amazement among His audience. A man, borne by four friends, had been let down through the roof of a house where Jesus was conducting a lecture. They had torn a hole in the roof because it would have been impossible to reach Jesus through the crowd. Jesus' first response to the man after acknowledging their faith was to forgive his sins. That elicited thoughts that Christ had blasphemed.

Christ had read the thoughts of his audience and responded to them. He declared that it was just as easy to heal the man. He then ordered the man to get up, take up his bed and walk.

The response of the Jews then had been different. In their amazement, they gave glory to God. They marveled that they had never seen it that way before.

*When Jesus saw their faith, he said unto the sick of the palsy, Son, thy sins be forgiven thee.*

*But there were certain of the scribes sitting there, and reasoning in their hearts, 'Why doth this man thus speak blasphemies? Who can forgive sins but God only?'*

*And immediately when Jesus perceived in his spirit that they so reasoned within themselves, he said unto them, 'Why reason ye these things in your hearts? Whether is it easier to say to the sick of the palsy, Thy sins be forgiven thee; or to say, Arise, and take up thy bed, and walk? But that ye may know that the Son of man hath power on earth to forgive sins, (he saith to the sick of the palsy,) I say unto thee, Arise, and take up thy bed, and go thy way into thine house'.*

*And immediately he arose, took up the bed, and went forth before them all; insomuch that they were all amazed, and glorified God, saying, We never saw it on this fashion* (Mk. 2:5 – 12).

Luke records the same incident with a little added flavor. In their amazement and act of glorifying God, they feared. They had reverence, not only for God the Father, but for Jesus also. They had never seen it that way before. That soon changed though.

*And when he saw their faith, he said unto him, Man, thy sins are forgiven thee.*

*And the scribes and the Pharisees began to reason, saying, 'Who is this which speaketh blasphemies? Who can forgive sins, but God alone?'*

*But when Jesus perceived their thoughts, he answering said unto them, 'What reason ye in your hearts?'*

*'Whether is easier, to say, Thy sins be forgiven thee; or to say, Rise up and walk? But that ye may know that the Son of man hath power upon earth to forgive sins, (he said unto the sick of the palsy,) I say unto thee, Arise, and take up thy couch, and go into thine house.'*

*And immediately he rose up before them, and took up that whereon he lay, and departed to his own house, glorifying God.*

*And they were all amazed, and they glorified God, and were filled with fear, saying, 'We have seen strange things to day'* (Lk. 5:20 – 26).

In John chapter eight, one has a classic example of the claims of Christ. He demonstrated who He was in every way. A quick browse through the chapter reveals at least eleven instances of Christ making claims in one way or the other.

The chapter opens with a crucial situation being brought to Jesus for adjudication. The expressed purpose was to fault Him and embarrass Him. Jesus knew their hearts and responded appropriately. Very early in the morning, the Scribes and Pharisees brought a woman to Jesus accusing that they had caught her in the act of adultery. They knew Moses had commanded that she be stoned but wanted Jesus to determine the matter. Interestingly, Jesus stooped down and wrote on the ground. At their insistence Jesus advised that the one without sin cast the first stone and He stooped again and continued writing.

One can only wonder at what Jesus wrote on the ground but that was enough to drive the fear of God into them. One after the other they filed away leaving the woman alone with Jesus. Soon Jesus stood up and asked about her accusers.

None had the moral rectitude to cast the first stone. Jesus' words to her were: *"Neither do I condemn thee: go, and sin no more."* He had again acted as God and had forgiven sin.

Jesus laid claim to being the light of the world and the Pharisees took objection. He bore record of Himself and the Pharisees quickly pounced on that seemingly unacceptable report of oneself to condemn Him. Jesus countered that His record was true because He knew where He had come from and that they did not know. That was a direct reference to His heavenly origin. He continued to contend that if He were to judge, His judgment would be true because of His connection with and to the Father.

Christ goes on to affirm that He bears witness of himself and the Father who sent Him bears witness of Him. That says that He is here on a mission from God. But the Pharisees queried His reference to the Father. "Where is your father?" They obviously thought He meant an earthly person. Jesus' reply was that you don't know Him because you don't know me. Christ's reference to 'he that sent me' is indicative of where He came from and that He had been in the presence of God.

Jesus now confounds those Pharisees with words that He would return to heaven. You can't come where I am going (paraphrased). Perplexed they asked whether He would kill himself. He again declares that they are from beneath (the earth) and He from above (heaven). Jesus further informs them that if they did not believe, they would die in their sins. That further puzzled them. "Who really are you?" asked the Pharisees, to which Jesus replied, "The same that I have always told you from the beginning."

Jesus goes on to intimate His death by crucifixion and that they would be the ones who would kill Him. After they had performed their dastardly act they would know the certainty of what He had said. He also confirmed that He always pleased the Father.

At that point many believed on Jesus. He reassured them that they would really be His disciples if they continued in the things that He said. They would know the truth and then they would really be free.

One of the most brutal of conversations ensued between Jesus and the Pharisees. There was serious dissonance regarding ancestral paternity. Jesus challenged them regarding their sin and their slavery to it. The only one who could afford them true freedom was the 'Son' – a direct reference to Himself. Until then they were the servants of sin. That demonstrated His position of authority and power with God while theirs was one of menial servitude to sin.

That elicited a vicious retort from the Pharisees regarding Christ's earthly paternity. To them Christ's paternity was questionable. They also claimed that they were legitimately the descendants of Abraham. To that Jesus countered that their attitudes and behavior belied their claimed parentage. Abraham would not seek to kill Him. The children of Abraham would not seek to kill Him. Their actions were proof positive that the Devil was their father. The difference in behavior between Him and them showed who their respective fathers were. Jesus was from God and they from the Devil. In no uncertain terms, Christ laid out the lifestyle of the Devil and showed them how theirs lined up with it. "You are of your father the Devil."

Jesus, in keeping with all of His other claims, now claims sinlessness. That He challenged them to convince or convict Him of. Of course to their chagrin, they could not honestly malign Him.

This claim is one that has touted Christ's divinity in a mighty way. Geisler expresses the power of that statement in these words:

"Simply living a sinless life, as difficult as that would be, would not necessarily prove someone is God. However, if someone both claims to be God and offers a sinless life as evidence that is an entirely different matter. All men are sinners; God knows it and so do we. If a man lives an impeccable life and offers as the truth about himself that he is God incarnated we must at least take his claim seriously. There are some who dare to claim perfection, but few take these claimants seriously, least of all those who know them best. With Jesus it is quite different; those who knew him best thought the most highly of him. Outsiders cast unsubstantiated allegations at him. "We are not born of fornication" [as you were] (John 8:41), or "he is leading the people astray" (John 7:12). Some even dared to say, "He has a demon, and is mad" (John 10:19). At his "trial" a false accusation brought forth that Jesus had said he would destroy the temple (Mark 14:58), "yet not even so did their testimony agree" (v. 59). Pilate's verdict as to Jesus' alleged crime has been the verdict of history as to his character: "I find no crime in this man" (Luke 23:4). The soldier at the cross exclaimed, "Certainly this man was innocent!" (Luke 23:47) and the dying thief, having earlier derided Christ (Matt. 27:39), came to see that "this man has done nothing wrong" and asked for a place in Jesus' kingdom (Luke 23:41, 42)."[50]

As the occasion presented itself, the Pharisees took another swipe at Christ's parentage. They called Him a Samaritan and accused Him of having a devil. Of course a Samaritan is a half Jew so they were in effect accusing Jesus of racial impurity, thus furthering their previous spurious sleight of words that they were not born of fornication. If he were of human patrimony, He could not be God.

Jesus continued to present His claims by declaring that they could have eternal life by keeping His words. They would never die. That made them the more irate in that, to them, a godly person like Abraham died; the prophets died; how can Jesus legitimately make the claim of eternal life? They could not understand.

Jesus then pointed out that He pre-existed Abraham. Abraham rejoiced to see His day. To the Jews, He was not even fifty years old yet and how could Abraham have rejoiced to see His day? Jesus ignited their hatred by claiming: "Before Abraham was, I am."

## Jesus claims to be the Father:

The Jews, though unbelieving, craved to know the reality about Jesus Christ. He had told them over and over again but they found it hard to accept the seemingly outlandish claims of Christ. They had in fact seen him grow before their eyes as any normal human being, yet He claimed heavenly origin. He lived among them doing the natural things that they all did, how, then, could He be God. They saw Him only as human. Apparently He had no airs about Him and His simplicity confounded them. Repeatedly they would ask the same question and get the same answers.

John records one occasion where Jesus not only claimed equality with the Father but actually claimed to be the Father. Here the Jews understood His claim and reacted with indignation. His statement was that in essence – His nature and in all other relevant characteristics – He was God.

*And Jesus walked in the temple in Solomon's porch.*

*Then came the Jews round about him, and said unto him, How long dost thou make us to doubt? If thou be the Christ, tell us plainly.*

*Jesus answered them, I told you, and ye believed not: the works that I do in my Father's name, they bear witness of me. But ye believe not, because ye are not of my sheep, as I said unto you.*

*My sheep hear my voice, and I know them, and they follow me: and I give unto them eternal life; and they shall never perish, neither shall any man pluck them out of my hand. My Father, which gave them me, is greater than all; and no man is able to pluck them out of my Father's hand. I and my Father are one.*

*Then the Jews took up stones again to stone him* (Jn. 10:23 – 31).

They well recognized, too, the magnitude of the claim considering the fact that God is one God. They were monotheistic and knew that Jesus knew the same. Indeed, He did, for He quoted their Scripture.

*Hear, O Israel: The LORD our God is one LORD: and thou shalt love the LORD thy God with all thine heart, and with all thy soul, and with all thy might* (Deut. 6:4, 5).

*And one of the scribes came, and having heard them reasoning together, and perceiving that he had answered them well, asked him, Which is the first commandment of all?*

*And Jesus answered him, The first of all the commandments is, Hear, O Israel; The Lord our God is one Lord: and thou shalt love the Lord thy God with all thy heart, and with all thy soul, and with all thy mind, and with all thy strength: this is the first commandment* (Mk. 12:28 - 30).

### Jesus was not deluded, neither was He ignorant:

On another occasion His disciples had a similar question. Although they had walked with Him for the past years and had witnessed all the miracles and heard all the teachings, they, too, had lingering doubts. It was simply unbelievable that God, a holy God would leave His heaven and cohabit with man. Yet, in all reality, that was what was happening right before their eyes. Here is the disciples' experience:

*Jesus saith unto him, I am the way, the truth, and the life: no man cometh unto the Father, but by me.*

> *If ye had known me, ye should have known my Father also: and from henceforth ye know him, and have seen him.*
>
> *Philip saith unto him, Lord, show us the Father, and it sufficeth us.*
>
> *Jesus saith unto him, Have I been so long time with you, and yet hast thou not known me, Philip? He that hath seen me hath seen the Father; and how sayest thou then, Show us the Father?* (Jn. 14:6 – 9).

Jesus was equally bold towards the Father. As has been said, Jesus knew the Scriptures. *I am the LORD: that is my name: and my glory will I not give to another, neither my praise to graven images* (Isa. 42:8). There was none on par with God and He shared His glory with no one.

Jesus, upon completion of His earthly ministry prayed something, which, if not true, was blasphemous. He addressed the Father thus: *And now, O Father, glorify thou me with thine own self with the glory which I had with thee before the world was* (Jn. 17:5). Christ could not have been deluded to request the Father to glorify Him with Himself. That was asking the Father to be God in place of Himself or alongside Him. But no, Christ knew that He shared equality with the Father before, and having finished His earthly mission was ready to resume His 'before Abraham was' position.

## Testimonies accepted by Jesus:

Jesus quizzed His disciples asking who men thought he was. To that the disciples gave many popular impressions of who Jesus was. Jesus then zeroed in on the disciples and wanted to know who they thought He was. After a moment's hesitation, Peter blurted out as only Peter could: "...*Thou art the Christ, the Son of the Living God*" (Mt. 15:16). To this Jesus replied: "...*Blessed art thou, Simon Barjona: for flesh and blood hath not revealed it unto thee, but my Father which is in heaven."* (Mt. 16:17) Jesus declared Peter's answer to be divine revelation.

The Christ is God's specially anointed Messenger anticipated by the Jews; one whom they expected to redeem Israel from the hands of their enemies. Jesus had quoted the Old Testament prophecy regarding the function of that Messiah at the beginning of His ministry when He read from Isaiah 61:1, 2 and had ascribed this to Himself. In His reply to the disciples of John, Jesus performed the miracles which would be associated with that Christ and had sent the disciples back to John to report what they had seen. Jesus knew and had accepted His role and functions in coming to the earth and was happy that at least His disciples had got it.

Later Jesus had another experience with His disciples. Jesus had resurrected and had appeared to His disciples, Thomas being absent. Thomas had been informed that Jesus had risen from the dead but determined not to believe unless he had concrete evidence. He must be able to put his fingers into the wounds that Jesus had sustained on the cross before he would concede that Jesus had indeed risen.

Eight days later, on the next Sunday, Jesus appears to His disciples – this time Thomas was there. Jesus invites Thomas to reach forward and feel the wounds. Who had informed Jesus of Thomas' statement? Did He know by intuition or had He known because He was God? Thomas did not then need the proof positive that he thought was necessary but acknowledged in a more forceful way than any of the other disciples had. He exclaimed: *"...My Lord and my God!"*

To declare Jesus Christ to be Lord was very profound. Jesus Christ being Lord ascribed to Him authority beyond measure. Jesus pronounced a blessing on all who would believe thereafter without having the evidence that Thomas had. One needs to accept by faith the fact that Jesus is Lord.

Not only did Thomas declare Him Lord, and rightly so, but Thomas recognized Jesus as God – his God. Jesus is not only the personal God of Thomas but God of the universe. God the Father has declared Jesus Christ to be Lord. Paul records the privilege of the Church as embodied in the person of Jesus Christ in the power God demonstrated in Him by His resurrection.

> *That the God of our Lord Jesus Christ, the Father of glory, may give unto you the spirit of wisdom and revelation in the knowledge of him: the eyes of your understanding being enlightened; that ye may know what is the hope of his calling, and what the riches of the glory of his inheritance in the saints, and what is the exceeding greatness of his power to us-ward who believe, according to the working of his mighty power, which he wrought in Christ, when he raised him from the dead, and set him at his own right hand in the heavenly places, far above all principality, and power, and might, and dominion, and every name that is named, not only in this world, but also in that which is to come: and hath put all things under his feet, and gave him to be the head over all things to the church, which is his body, the fullness of him that filleth all in all (Eph. 1:17 – 23).*

**Christ's power is also recorded by Peter in this way:**

> *For the eyes of the Lord are over the righteous, and his ears are open unto their prayers: but the face of the Lord is against them that do evil (I Pet. 3:12).*

Paul accounts for the position of Jesus Christ in this way:

*Wherefore God also hath highly exalted him, and given him a name which is above every name: that at the name of Jesus every knee should bow, of things in heaven, and things in earth, and things under the earth; and that every tongue should confess that Jesus Christ is Lord, to the glory of God the Father (Phil. 2:9 – 11).*

# CHAPTER SEVEN

# THE CLAIMS OF CHRIST - PART 2

Jesus Christ, the founder of the Christian religion, lays some powerful claims which leave Christianity in a category all by itself. No other religious leader has made the claims that Jesus made and fulfilled them. No other founder has even dared to make some of the claims that Jesus made. Christianity is unique and alone in its tenets and practices. While most other religions will present their beliefs in ways which may not take into account the existence of other religions, Christianity makes absolute declarations which discount all others and establishes an exclusivity which only a founder like Jesus Christ could claim and uphold. Christianity deals in specifics rather than in generalities which would leave room for others. It is obvious that the plethora of religions and denominations and cults and sects are not of God although there are some sub groupings which carry a variety of names yet hold to the basic doctrines of Christianity.

The basic teachings of Christianity include: the doctrine of the trinity; the universality of sin, the total depravity of man and his inability to save himself; salvation by grace through faith in the vicarious substitutionary death of Jesus Christ for and on behalf of man; a life sanctified unto God because of the justification procured and administered by Jesus Christ; a future hope of eternal life with Christ; eternal damnation for those who would reject God's free gift of salvation; faith in the plenary inspiration of and the inerrancy of the Bible. There are other teachings, corollary to those basic doctrines, where denominations vary and follow practices which neither add to nor take away from the truth of the Gospel. Paul presents the message of the Gospel simply as: *"For I delivered unto you first of all that which I also received, how that Christ died for our sins according to the scriptures; and that he was buried, and that he rose again the third day according to the scriptures:"* (I cor. 15:3, 4). The sum total of the Gospel then would be the death, burial and resurrection of Jesus Christ. One example of a variation is the regularity with which communion is observed. The important thing is that it is observed.

Jesus Christ presented the Gospel, among other things, in the emphatic "I am" of the New Testament. These have direct correlation to the "I am that I am" which God expressed to Moses as the one who had sent him to deliver Israel from Egyptian bondage. In presenting Himself in this way, He does not only emphasize His Old Testament identity but puts His stamp of exclusivity in the affairs of man.

In presenting Himself as the "I Am" Jesus was laying claim to His self-existence. It was He who said: *"Therefore doth my Father love me, because I lay down my life, that I might take it again. No man taketh it from me, but I lay it down of myself. I have power to lay it down, and I have power to take it again. This commandment have I received of my Father."* (Jn. 10:17. 18) On another occasion Jesus repeated His claim: *"For as the Father hath life in himself; so hath he given to the Son to have life in himself; and hath given him authority to execute judgment also, because he is the Son of man.* (Jn. 5:26, 27)

Another thing Jesus Christ did was declare that He is ever present. He existed before His birth and continues to exist after His death. He is, as the Psalmist records Moses to have prayed, *"Before the mountains were brought forth, or ever thou hadst formed the earth and the world, even from everlasting to everlasting, thou art God"* (Ps. 90:2). We are reminded in John 1:1 that it was Jesus who created. How could the Psalmist not have been referring to Him also? Jesus continually told His hearers that after His departure from this world He was going to be with the Father. He was going to prepare a place for them. He was coming back to take His disciples to be with Him forever. He is the ever existing one.

### The exclusivity of Jesus' claims:

Among the "I Am" of Jesus is this one that we deal with first. In John 14:6, Jesus says to Thomas: *"I am the way, the truth, and the life: no man cometh unto the Father, but by me."* One needs to carefully examine this passage to see what Jesus is claiming here. We have seen that, in His use of the emphatic, Jesus has made particular claims which are no different here. But the claims do not end with His existence. They continue into His essential being and mission.

Three times in this short passage we see Christ using the 'definite article'. Now the article is a word used in grammar to indicate the definiteness of the noun it precedes. It is used as an adjective and qualifies the noun that follows. In our English language there are basically two articles – the definite article "the" and the indefinite article "a" or "an" when used before a word beginning with a vowel. "a" indicates one of many and defines the noun appropriately. "the" on the other hand indicates that whatever is identified is the one and only. An example of this is to use an article before the word 'book'. To say 'a book' recognizes that there are many of the same type or of varying ilk. To say "the book" singles out a particular book as the one to which reference is made. A dictionary definition of an article is:

An **article** (abbreviated ART) is a word that combines with a noun to indicate the type of reference being made by the noun. Articles specify the grammatical definiteness of the noun, in some languages extending to volume or numerical scope.[51]

Jesus addresses Himself as "the" in three different spheres. In so doing He limits those spheres to Himself alone. That precludes any other and restricts the number to the one and only. Jesus Christ is **the** way, **the** truth and **the** life. It does one well to examine each of these exclusives a little more and to come to terms with the reality of each claim in the light of the vast number of religious denominations around. The Apostle Paul says: *"But though we, or an angel from heaven, preach any other gospel unto you than that which we have preached unto you, let him be accursed"* (Gal. 1:8). It is incumbent on each and every person to ascertain the truth, not according to his denomination, but according to the Word of God.

Before considering the three exclusives of this verse let us pay some attention to the rest of the prohibition. Jesus declares that "no man" can come to the Father but through Him. That prohibits every single person who has lived or is living upon the earth. Not an one can come to the Father unless He comes through Jesus Christ. That enjoins the next prohibition in that the purpose and ultimate end of man seems to be to get to the Father. Most religions have an eternal hope whether it is to experience nirvana or reincarnation or any other form of after life experience. There is no other acceptable after life experience than to live with the Father in His house. No one can get to him but through Jesus Christ.

Enclosed in that prohibition is another astounding truth. Jesus says, "No man cometh unto the Father". Important in this phrase is the direction of movement – can come. It denotes movement in the direction of the speaker. That indicates that Jesus is either in the same locality as the Father or that the Father is in some location behind Jesus. Because one understands the relationship between the Father and the Son one knows that one is coming to the same person. One realizes, too, that the means through which God has ordained that the gap between Him and man be bridged is through the physical human representation of Himself. God has declared, too, that anyone who will not acknowledge the Son does not acknowledge Him.

> *Beloved, believe not every spirit, but try the spirits whether they are of God: because many false prophets are gone out into the world. Hereby know ye the Spirit of God: Every spirit that <u>confesseth that Jesus Christ is come in the flesh</u> is of God: and every spirit that <u>confesseth not that Jesus Christ is come in the flesh</u> is not of God: and this is that spirit of antichrist, whereof ye have heard that it should come; and even now already is it in the world* (Jn. 4:1 – 3).

> *For there is one God, and one mediator between God and men<u>, the man Christ Jesus</u>; who gave himself a ransom for all, to be testified in due time* (I Tim 2:5, 6). (underline mine)

Such access to the Father and the privileges of the Christian is expressed also in Hebrews as navigating through the 'Temple'. Access into the most holy place was through the veil which is comparative to the body of Jesus Christ. Whereas in the Temple the veil was to restrict access into the

Most Holy Place, Christ's body, having been broken on the cross, allows free access to the Most Holy One.

> *Having therefore, brethren, boldness to enter into the holiest by the blood of Jesus, by a new and living way, which he hath consecrated for us, <u>through the veil, that is to say, his flesh</u>; and having an high priest over the house of God; let us draw near with a true heart in full assurance of faith, having our hearts sprinkled from an evil conscience, and our bodies washed with pure water* (Heb. 10:19 – 22). (underline mine)

## I am the way:

Having established the definiteness of the claim of Jesus Christ, let us look at "the way". We have seen briefly some of the claims of other parts of the Scripture, but what does Jesus say about His being the way?

> *Then said Jesus again unto them, I go my way, and ye shall seek me, and shall die in your sins: whither I go, ye cannot come (Jn. 8:21).*

Jesus was speaking to the Jews and confounded them with His sayings. They did not understand the fact that He had to go neither did they know where He was going. Jesus, at that time, did not elucidate to the Pharisees but left them to wonder. This verse must be understood though in the light of what Jesus said to His disciples later. They, too, had some queries regarding the way. To them Jesus said:

> *'And whither I go ye know, and the way ye know.'*
> *Thomas saith unto him, 'Lord, we know not whither thou goest; and how can we know the way?'*

*Jesus saith unto him, 'I am the way, the truth, and the life: no man cometh unto the Father, but by me'* (Jn. 14: 4 – 6).

Salvation is by grace through faith in the work which Christ accomplished on the cross. He took the punishment for man's sin which was death and offers life to all who will believe in Him. Jesus said to Nicodemus three times that the rebirth experience is an absolute necessity if one is to enter the kingdom of God. *"You must be born again"* (Jn. 3:3, 5, 7). It is an imperative which applies to all who will come to God. *"That which is born of the flesh is flesh; and that which is born of the Spirit is spirit."* One realizes through this statement that there are two births – a physical birth and a spiritual birth. One must come into that spiritual birth relationship with God by simply believing in Jesus Christ and what he achieved for us through His death.

Man, at creation, was created perfect (sinless) and had fellowship with God. When sin entered, because of Adam's disobedience to God's command, that perfection was lost and the relationship between God and man was broken.

*Wherefore, as by one man sin entered into the world, and death by sin; and so death passed upon all men, for that all have sinned: (For until the law sin was in the world: but sin is not imputed when there is no law Nevertheless death reigned from Adam to Moses, even over them that had not sinned after the similitude of Adam's transgression, who is the figure of him that was to come.*

*But not as the offence, so also is the free gift. For if through the offence of one many be dead, much more the grace of God, and the gift by grace, which is by one man, Jesus Christ, hath abounded unto many.*

*And not as it was by one that sinned, so is the gift: for the judgment was by one to condemnation, but the free gift is of many offences unto justification. For if by one man's offence death reigned by one; much more they which receive abundance of grace and of the gift of righteousness shall reign in life by one, Jesus Christ.)*

*Therefore as by the offence of one judgment came upon all men to condemnation; even so by the righteousness of one the free gift came upon all men unto justification of life. For as by one man's disobedience many were made sinners, so by the obedience of one shall many be made righteous* (Rom. 5:12 – 19).

Ever since that time, man has sought through every means possible to get back into that relationship with God. It is because of that quest that man has established religions. But the relationship can be restored simply and only by faith in Christ who is **the way** back.

*And as Moses lifted up the serpent in the wilderness, even so must the Son of man be lifted up: that whosoever believeth in him should not perish, but have eternal life.*

*For God so loved the world, that he gave his only begotten Son, that whosoever believeth in him should not perish, but have everlasting life.*

*For God sent not his Son into the world to condemn the world; but that the world through him might be saved.*

*He that believeth on him is not condemned: but he that believeth not is condemned already, because he hath not believed in the name of the only begotten Son of God. And this is the condemnation, that light is come into the world, and men loved darkness rather than light, because their deeds were evil* (Jn. 3:14 – 19).

*He that believeth on the Son hath everlasting life: and he that believeth not the Son shall not see life; but the wrath of God abideth on him* (Jn. 3:36).

*For the Father judgeth no man, but hath committed all judgment unto the Son: that all men should honour the Son, even as they honour the Father. He that honoureth not the Son honoureth not the Father which hath sent him.*
   *Verily, verily, I say unto you, He that heareth my word, and believeth on him that sent me, hath everlasting life, and shall not come into condemnation; but is passed from death unto life* (Jn. 5:22 – 24).

*But as many as received him, to them gave he power to become the sons of God, even to them that believe on his name: which were born, not of blood, nor of the will of the flesh, nor of the will of man, but of God* (Jn. 1:12, 13).

**Jesus is the only way back to God.**

Christ uses two other symbolisms which depict that access to the Father is only through Him. These symbols are ones that the people of His day well understood the significance of. Today, modernization has left us without physical understanding of what Christ referred to but history assists in understanding what was meant. Animals were herded and contained by enclosing them in a fenced area or coral. Today's coral may be a replica of what persisted then. There was only one entrance to that enclosure and the shepherd or herdsman would lie across that entrance to guard it. Any one or any wild animal would have to gain access through that entrance. In this way the guardian would know what went in or what came out.

Jesus used this to bring home the point that He was the only means of access to the Father and to life.

*Verily, verily, I say unto you, He that entereth not by the door into the sheepfold, but climbeth up some other way, the same is a thief and a robber.*

*But he that entereth in by the door is the shepherd of the sheep.*

*Then said Jesus unto them again, Verily, verily, I say unto you, <u>I am the door of the sheep.</u>*

*<u>I am the door</u>: by me if any man enters in, he shall be saved, and shall go in and out, and find pasture* (Jn. 10:1, 2, 7, 9). (underline mine)

*Then said one unto him, Lord, are there few that be saved?*

*And he said unto them, "Strive to enter in at the strait gate: for many, I say unto you, will seek to enter in, and shall not be able. When once the master of the house is risen up, and hath shut to the door, and ye begin to stand without, and to knock at the door, saying, Lord, Lord, open unto us; and he shall answer and say unto you, I know you not whence ye are: then shall ye begin to say, 'We have eaten and drunk in thy presence, and thou hast taught in our streets.' But he shall say, I tell you, I know you not whence ye are; depart from me, all ye workers of iniquity. There shall be weeping and gnashing of teeth, when ye shall see Abraham, and Isaac, and Jacob, and all the prophets, in the kingdom of God, and you yourselves thrust out.*

*And they shall come from the east, and from the west, and from the north, and from the south, and shall sit down in the kingdom of God* (Lk. 13:23 – 29).

*But after that the kindness and love of God our Saviour toward man appeared, Not by works of righteousness which we have done, but according to his mercy he saved us, by the washing of regeneration, and renewing of the Holy Ghost; which he shed on us abundantly through Jesus Christ our Saviour; that being justified by his grace, we should be made heirs according to the hope of eternal life* (Tit. 3:4 – 7).

*For the preaching of the cross is to them that perish foolishness; but unto us which are saved it is the power of God.*
*Where is the wise? Where is the scribe? Where is the disputer of this world? Hath not God made foolish the wisdom of this world?*
*For after that in the wisdom of God the world by wisdom knew not God, it pleased God, by the foolishness of preaching, to save them that believe.*
*For the Jews require a sign, and the Greeks seek after wisdom: But we preach Christ crucified, unto the Jews a stumbling block, and unto the Greeks foolishness; but unto them which are called, both Jews and Greeks, Christ the power of God, and the wisdom of God. Because the foolishness of God is wiser than men; and the weakness of God is stronger than men* (I Cor. 1:18, 20 – 25).

Every religion which does not recognize Jesus Christ as the only way is false and every religion which offers Jesus Christ plus anything else is deceitful.

**I am the truth:**

"What is truth?"

This is a question that Pilate asked Jesus as He stood before him, delivered by the Jews to be condemned. Pilate's query was whether Jesus was indeed the king of the Jews. Jesus, in usual fashion had indicated that He had come to bear witness of the truth and those who are of the truth accept Him. They believe that He is who He says He is and believe the message He declares to them.

> *Then Pilate entered into the judgment hall again, and called Jesus, and said unto him, Art thou the King of the Jews?*
>
> *Jesus answered him, Sayest thou this thing of thyself, or did others tell it thee of me?*
>
> *Pilate answered, Am I a Jew? Thine own nation and the chief priests have delivered thee unto me: what hast thou done?*
>
> *Jesus answered, My kingdom is not of this world: if my kingdom were of this world, then would my servants fight, that I should not be delivered to the Jews: but now is my kingdom not from hence.*
>
> *Pilate therefore said unto him, Art thou a king then? Jesus answered, Thou sayest that I am a king. To this end was I born, and for this cause came I into the world, that I should bear witness unto the truth. Every one that is of the truth heareth my voice.*
> *Pilate saith unto him, What is truth? And when he had said this, he went out again unto the Jews, and saith unto them, I find in him no fault at all* (Jn. 18:33 – 38).

If, as Jesus Christ declared, what He spoke was the truth, then there is no room for other doctrines or religious beliefs. One cannot find another philosophy or any other belief system which would approximate what Jesus taught for there is no other. Truth is truth and any departure from that constitutes a lie.

John, under the inspiration of the Holy Spirit, wrote in commentary and direct quotation the truth regarding Jesus' truth. He says:

> *And the Word was made flesh, and dwelt among us, (and we beheld his glory, the glory as of the only begotten of the Father,) full of grace and truth.*
> *For the law was given by Moses, but grace and truth came by Jesus Christ* (Jn. 1:14, 17).

John should know because He was one of the first disciples Jesus called. He was one of the inner circle and was always with Jesus. He attests that his information is firsthand information which, from all indications, is incontestable. His information is:

> *That which was from the beginning, which we have heard, which we have seen with our eyes, which we have looked upon, and our hands have handled, of the Word of life; (For the life was manifested, and we have seen it, and bear witness, and show unto you that eternal life, which was with the Father, and was manifested unto us;) That which we have seen and heard declare we unto you, that ye also may have fellowship with us: and truly our fellowship is with the Father, and with his Son Jesus Christ* (I Jn. 1:1 – 3).

John's information is not hearsay from a reporter or third party but is what he heard himself. He had personal information that only a select few of them had. It was he and two others, Peter and James, who were on the Mount of

Transfiguration with Jesus when He was transfigured before them. They saw Moses and Elijah. They heard the voice declare the identity of Jesus. They saw the radiance of God who spoke from the cloud.

> *And after six days Jesus taketh Peter, James, and John his brother, and bringeth them up into an high mountain apart, and was transfigured before them: and his face did shine as the sun, and his raiment was white as the light. And, behold, there appeared unto them Moses and Elias talking with him.*
>
> *Then answered Peter, and said unto Jesus, Lord, it is good for us to be here: if thou wilt, let us make here three tabernacles; one for thee, and one for Moses, and one for Elias.*
>
> *While he yet spake, behold, a bright cloud overshadowed them: and behold a voice out of the cloud, which said, This is my beloved Son, in whom I am well pleased; hear ye him* (Mt. 17:1 – 5).

Pilate asked a very poignant question when he asked, "What is truth?" Man continues to ask the same question although it has been answered and is easily answered from the Word of God. But again, truth may take on different characteristics depending on the sphere or subject to which it is related. Not that truth changes but the limitations of knowledge and availability of relevant information color the conclusions one may arrive at. Wikipedia defines truth as:

**Truth** can have a variety of meanings, such as the state of being in accord with a particular fact or reality, or being in accord with the body of real things, real events or actualities. It can also mean having fidelity to an original or to a standard or ideal. In a common archaic usage it also meant constancy or sincerity in action or character.

The direct opposite of truth is "falsehood", which can correspondingly take logical, factual or ethical meanings.

However, language and words are essentially "tools" by which humans convey information to one another. As such, "truth" must have a beneficial use in order to be retained within language. Since truths are used in planning and prediction (such as scientific truths being used in engineering), the more reliable and trustworthy an idea is, the more useful and potent it becomes for planning and prediction. Those ideas which can be used anywhere and anytime with maximum reliability are generally considered the most powerful and potent truths. Defining this potency and applicability can be looked upon as "criteria", and the method used to recognize a "truth" is termed a criteria of truth. Since there is no single accepted criteria, they can all be considered "theories".

Various theories and views of truth continue to be debated among scholars and philosophers. There are differing claims on such questions as what constitutes truth; what things are truthbearers capable of being true or false; how to define and identify truth; the roles that revealed and acquired knowledge play; and whether truth is subjective, relative, objective, or absolute. This article introduces the various perspectives and claims, both today and throughout history.[52]

This definition, from a human perspective is very truthful. It is a very practical working definition of the sciences and anything of human origin. One thing it does not outrightly declare is that an absolute being must of necessity have absolute truth. God is an absolute being. Jesus Christ declares there is a God and claims to be God. Anything Jesus declares or gives assent to must, of necessity, be truth. Therefore, Jesus' claim that He is "the truth" is an absolute declaration of truth.

*Jesus saith unto him, I am the way, the truth, and the life: no man cometh unto the Father, but by me.*

*If ye love me, keep my commandments. And I will pray the Father, and he shall give you another Comforter, that he may abide with you for ever; even the Spirit of truth; whom the world cannot receive, because it seeth him not, neither knoweth him: but ye know him; for he dwelleth with you, and shall be in you* (Jn. 14:6, 15 – 17).

Jesus Christ did not just exist and exit this world leaving a historical blur for today's generation but insists that He will send the Holy Spirit, who is another of the same ilk as He, to be with man and in man. The lack of experience on the part of some does not constitute the nonexistence of the Holy Spirit but the continuous consistent experience of those who are disposed to receiving truth does constitute the truthfulness of what Jesus said. Experiences, though individualistic, are of such a consistent nature that it removes itself from being simply subjective to a level of objectivity that it is acceptable. A wide variety of persons cannot experience the same thing simply by willing themselves to, but can experience the same thing if that thing is a reality. Jesus said that the Holy Spirit, though a spirit and unseen, can and will be experienced. As a matter of fact, both Christ and the Father will accompany the Holy Spirit. (Jn. 12:23 - *Jesus answered and said unto him, If a man love me, he will keep my words: and my Father will love him, and **we** will come unto him, and make **our** abode with him*).

## Some logical insights:

As has been seen in the above definition, there are parameters within which truth will operate. Truth cannot be arbitrary or subjective but must be within particular frameworks which will allow it to be public and objective. It must be able to work regardless of who operates in it. We glean the following insights (the full text not quoted) from a logistician Norman L. Geisler:

"...there is a characteristic commonality in the evidential appeal that bears exposition and evaluation.

1. First evidentialism is empirically or experientially based... Truth must be based in facts, not in ideas or theories, or else it is not grounded at all. Truth is based in facts or events.

2. It is possible to relate and structure many, if not all, facts in differing ways. But the interpretation does not constitute the facts. Facts stand by themselves apart from frameworks that may be given to them from differing points of view.

3. To be sure, facts need interpretation but the interpretation cannot be arbitrarily imposed from without; rather, it arises from the facts themselves in a natural way.

4. Evidentialists often appeal to some special or unique facts as being definitive in determining truth. For some it may be past miraculous events, for others it may be a present mystical experience, and for still others it may be a final blessed state. Christians most often appeal to the fact of the incarnation, to the crucial events of the life of Jesus, as definitive for truth.

5. Many evidentialists place strong emphasis on the objective and public nature of facts. In this respect they regard private and subjective experience as nonevidential. Truth must be observable and general or it is unsubstantiatable.[53]

In light of the above insights, the facts that Jesus made the statements that He is reported to have made must be taken in the context that Jesus did live. The statements were made to and of persons who were alive at the time and could have disproved the reports. The recorded events and statements were reported by eye witnesses who themselves were guided by the Holy Spirit of Truth. These statements are worthy of due consideration.

Jesus continued to make statements regarding the truth:

> But he that doeth truth cometh to the light, that his deeds may be made manifest, that they are wrought in God (Jn. 3:21).

> If I bear witness of myself, my witness is not true. There is another that beareth witness of me; and I know that the witness which he witnesseth of me is true. Ye sent unto John, and he bare witness unto the truth (Jn. 5: 31 – 33).

> Therefore they gathered them together, and filled twelve baskets with the fragments of the five barley loaves, which remained over and above unto them that had eaten. Then those men, when they had seen the miracle that Jesus did, said, 'This is of a truth that prophet that should come into the world' (Jn. 6:13, 14).

> And what he hath seen and heard, that he testifieth; and no man receiveth his testimony. He that hath received his testimony hath set to his seal that God is true. For he whom God hath sent speaketh the words of God: for God giveth not the Spirit by measure unto him (Jn. 3:32 – 34).

Others testified of Jesus that He was true and that He was the Truth.

*In the last day, that great day of the feast, Jesus stood and cried, saying, If any man thirst, let him come unto me, and drink. He that believeth on me, as the scripture hath said, out of his belly shall flow rivers of living water. (But this spake he of the Spirit, which they that believe on him should receive: for the Holy Ghost was not yet given; because that Jesus was not yet glorified.) Many of the people therefore, when they heard this saying, said, Of a truth this is the Prophet (Jn. 7:37 – 40).*

*That was the true Light, which lighteth every man that cometh into the world* (Jn. 1:9).

*And they sent out unto him their disciples with the Herodians, saying, Master, we know that thou art true, and teachest the way of God in truth, neither carest thou for any man: for thou regardest not the person of men* (Mt. 22:16).

*A minister of the sanctuary, and of the true tabernacle, which the Lord pitched, and not man* (Heb. 8:2).

*For Christ is not entered into the holy places made with hands, which are the figures of the true; but into heaven itself, now to appear in the presence of God for us: nor yet that he should offer himself often, as the high priest entereth into the holy place every year with blood of others; for then must he often have suffered since the foundation of the world: but now once in the end of the world hath he appeared to put away sin by the sacrifice of himself* (Heb. 9:24 – 26).

*And we know that the Son of God is come, and hath given us an understanding, that we may know him that is true, and we are in him that is true, even in his Son Jesus Christ. This is the true God, and eternal life* (I Jn. 5:20).

Jesus said: "I am the truth." This statement excludes every other message. Only Christianity carries truth, for all truth is found in Christ and only in Christ.

## I am the life:

Jesus' third exclusive claim is to being **the Life.** Life as we know it came from God. Genesis records that God breathed into man and man came alive. Life therefore is the breath of God. It is He who gives and it is He who takes away. This is one of the reasons that one should not kill (except with permission from God - Governments). Christ's claim to being God makes Him also the giver of life. His claim to being life makes Him God.

*In whom we have redemption through his blood, even the forgiveness of sins: who is the image of the invisible God, the firstborn of every creature: for by him were all things created, that are in heaven, and that are in earth, visible and invisible, whether they be thrones, or dominions, or principalities, or powers: all things were created by him, and for him: and he is before all things, and by him all things consist. And he is the head of the body, the church: who is the beginning, the firstborn from the dead; that in all things he might have the preeminence* (Col. 1:14 – 18).

Life does not only concern our existence through each day, but includes our eternal existence after the death of the body. The Bible speaks of the wages for sin as death. There are two aspects to death just as there are two aspects to life. There is a physical death where the body ceases to live and readily decomposes to dust from which it was taken. But there is also spiritual death which took place when man became a sinner. That death is separation from God. Man in his sinful condition is separated from God now. Man who dies in his sinful condition experiences the second aspect of death, which is separation from God for all eternity. Whether Christian or non-Christian, man continues to exist for all eternity. Where one spends eternity is the business of one's life here.

It is for this reason that God says firstly that the wages of sin is death. Because of one man's sin all men are sinners and therefore under the condemnation of sin which is separation from God. Romans 5:12 tells us: *"Wherefore, as by one man sin entered into the world, and death by sin; and so death passed upon all men, for that all have sinned."* Generically, man is a sinner because man inherited it from Adam. Practically, every man, because of his inherent sinful nature, commits sin. Man lives in continuous rebellion against God's laws therefore he is under continuous condemnation. When man acknowledges his sinful condition and repents, asking God's forgiveness; turns away from his sin and reposes full confidence in the death of Jesus Christ as adequate payment for his sin, man becomes a saint in the eyes of God. The Bible says: *"Verily, verily, I say unto you, He that heareth my word, and believeth on him that sent me, hath everlasting life, and shall not come into condemnation; but is passed from death unto life"* (Jn. 5:24). Man then obtains a new lease on life. This is the Christian's contention and the fundamental difference between itself and other religions. Christians have the hope of living forever with God in His kingdom. The work is fully and completely that of Christ – God's provision for man. God's word says:

> *"Wherefore, as by one man sin entered into the world, and death by sin; and so death passed upon all men, for that all have sinned: (For until the law sin*

*was in the world: but sin is not imputed when there is no law. Nevertheless death reigned from Adam to Moses, even over them that had not sinned after the similitude of Adam's transgression, who is the figure of him that was to come.*

*But not as the offence, so also is the free gift. For if through the offence of one many be dead, much more the grace of God, and the gift by grace, which is by one man, Jesus Christ, hath abounded unto many.*

*And not as it was by one that sinned, so is the gift: for the judgment was by one to condemnation, but the free gift is of many offences unto justification. For if by one man's offence death reigned by one; much more they which receive abundance of grace and of the gift of righteousness shall reign in life by one, Jesus Christ.)*

*Therefore as by the offence of one judgment came upon all men to condemnation; even so by the righteousness of one the free gift came upon all men unto justification of life. For as by one man's disobedience many were made sinners, so by the obedience of one shall many be made righteous"* (Rom. 5:12 - 19).

God's provision for man is a free gift. The cost of this gift made it so prohibitive that man could not afford it. It required the shedding of the blood of one who was perfectly sinless and propitiatory in order to atone for the sins of man. God says of man: "... *There is none righteous, no not one"* (Rom. 3:10). That puts the requirement for reconciliation beyond the capability of mortal man. Again each man and each act of sin carried the penalty of death. There was none able to pay, for each has only one life. Only God in His perfection and in the form of mortal man could pay the price of man's sin and still have life to continue a meaningful relationship with man.

Consequently, for man to benefit from that provision, it had to be free. For that reason, too, God will accept no human effort as satisfactory for man's debt of sin.

> *Being justified freely by his grace through the redemption that is in Christ Jesus: whom God hath set forth to be <u>a propitiation</u> through faith in his blood, to declare his righteousness for the remission of sins that are past, through the forbearance of God; to declare, I say, at this time his righteousness: that he might be just, and the justifier of him which believeth in Jesus* (Rom. 3:24 – 26).

> *My little children, these things write I unto you, that ye sin not. And if any man sin, we have an advocate with the Father, Jesus Christ the righteous: and he is <u>the propitiation</u> for our sins: and not for ours only, but also for the sins of the whole world* (I Jn. 2:1, 2).

> *In this was manifested the love of God toward us, because that God sent his only begotten Son into the world, that we might live through him. Herein is love, not that we loved God, but that he loved us, and sent his Son to be <u>the propitiation</u> for our sins* (I Jn. 4:9, 10). (underline mine)

The Father endorsed the claims of Christ so it is with legitimacy that Christ continues to claim exclusivity regarding life. Christ continues to say:

> *Verily, verily, I say unto you, He that heareth my word, and believeth on him that sent me, hath everlasting life, and shall not come into condemnation; but is passed from death unto life* (Jn. 5:24).

*Search the scriptures; for in them ye think ye have eternal life: and they are they which testify of me* (Jn. 5:39).

*And Jesus said unto them, I am the bread of life: he that cometh to me shall never hunger; and he that believeth on me shall never thirst* (Jn. 6:35).

There are other Scripture which attest to the fact that Christ is life and in Him there is life. John, the writer who declares the divinity of Jesus Christ most profusely, declares:

*In him was life; and the life was the light of men* (Jn. 1:4).

*That whosoever believeth in him should not perish, but have eternal life. For God so loved the world, that he gave his only begotten Son, that whosoever believeth in him should not perish, but have everlasting life* (Jn. 3:15, 16).

*He that believeth on the Son hath everlasting life: and he that believeth not the Son shall not see life; but the wrath of God abideth on him* (Jn. 3:36).

*For as the Father hath life in himself; so hath he given to the Son to have life in himself; and hath given him authority to execute judgment also, because he is the Son of man. Marvel not at this: for the hour is coming, in the which all that are in the graves shall hear his voice, and shall come forth; they that have done good, unto the resurrection of life; and they that have done evil, unto the resurrection of damnation* (Jn. 5:26 – 29).

*Jesus said unto her, I am the resurrection, and the life: he that believeth in me, though he were dead, yet shall he live: and whosoever liveth and believeth in me shall never die* (Jn. 11:25, 26).

*I will not leave you comfortless: I will come to you. Yet a little while, and the world seeth me no more; but ye see me: because I live, ye shall live also. At that day ye shall know that I am in my Father, and ye in me, and I in you.* (Jn. 14:18 – 20)

The definiteness of Jesus and His teaching was not limited to only the three expressed in John 14:6 but extends to every vital aspect of the life of a believer. Many claim to have knowledge and understanding but even there Christ claims exclusivity. *"Then spake Jesus again unto them, saying, I am the light of the world: he that followeth me shall not walk in darkness, but shall have the light of life"* (Jn. 8:12). Light here is not restricted to the perception of color or the rays of the sun or artificial lighting but to knowledge and understanding. Knowledge comes in when understanding takes place. Such experience is often referred to as "seeing the light". Words may be read or heard but until there is perception there is no communication.

John Hayford, in one of his television messages shared some very powerful insights into the resurrection of Jesus when he spoke of the disciples' entry into the seemingly empty tomb of Jesus. After receiving the news that the tomb was opened and Jesus was not there Peter and John ran to the sepulchre to find that it was so. From outside looking in John saw the grave clothes lying there. The body was not there. But when Peter, who came after, entered the sepulchre he, too, entered. The Bible says that: *"Then went in also that other disciple, which came first to the sepulchre, and he saw, and believed."* What does the Scripture mean, *"...he saw, and believed?*" Had he not seen from the doorway? What John saw was not only what entered the eye gate but perception elucidated his intellect.

John saw the clothes lying there. It was an empty shell of what had previously enclosed the body of Jesus. It was not tampered with. It was obvious that the lack of a body was not the result of a theft. The body had exited the clothes leaving it in the exact shape of the body that it had wrapped. Jesus had indeed resurrected and left the empty wrapping as testimony of that fact.

John saw, too, the napkin which was around the head of Jesus, folded and well placed apart from what had covered the body of Jesus. The folded napkin was a matter of great cultural significance. In those days masters were served by their servants and the position of the napkin was very meaningful. When a master was finished eating, he would wad up the napkin and place it on the plate. That indicated that his meal was complete. If a master were to leave the table before he was finished, he would carefully fold the napkin and place it beside the plate indicating that he was coming back to the table and his meal. John saw the napkin which had wrapped the head of Jesus carefully folded and properly positioned in relation to the other wrappings. That indicated that Jesus meant to come back. He was not stolen away, he left. This is why the angels invited the ladies in Matthew 28:6, *"He is not here: for he is risen, as he said. Come, see the place where the Lord lay."*

John more than saw the clothes lying there; he had insight into what had happened. This is the light of which Jesus speaks. He is light. He brings understanding and there is no need to wallow in the darkness of ignorance. *"The entrance of thy words giveth light; it giveth understanding unto the simple."* (Ps. 119:130) The Psalmist, hundreds of years before the time of Christ, had that understanding. John tells us: *"And this is the condemnation, that light is come into the world, and men loved darkness rather than light, because their deeds were evil. For every one that doeth evil hateth the light, neither cometh to the light, lest his deeds should be reproved"* (Jn. 3:19, 20).

Man is willfully ignorant. Christ said: *"As long as I am in the world, I am the light of the world."* (Jn. 9:5) Christ is now in heaven but His words are still with us. The Bible is hated because of its capacity to expose. Christians, too, are hated because of the same effect that their presence has in the world. Jesus said again:

> *Ye are the light of the world. A city that is set on an hill cannot be hid. Neither do men light a candle, and put it under a bushel, but on a candlestick; and it giveth light unto all that are in the house. Let your light so shine before men, that they may see your good works, and glorify your Father which is in heaven* (Mt. 5:14 – 16).

Christians bear light, not only by the life they live but by the message they carry. Even as Christ declared the words of God, Christians, too, are to declare the same. Paul uses the phrase *"I declare unto you that which I also received."* That should be the mantra of all Christians for the message is not original with each individual but a relaying of that which is written. Christianity is not an evolving organization but an organism founded and centered in the light which Christ is.

Christ also refers to Himself as the Good Shepherd. Here, His care and provision for those who are His, is indicated. As a shepherd He leads His followers and protects them from the wiles of the enemy. Both physical and spiritual protection are proffered; although, for His own purposes, He may allow the destruction of the body by the enemy. He emphatically declares His protection over those who are His. In contrast to the hireling, He promises never to leave or forsake His flock. Though, one may think to ridicule the thought of protection and the allowing of physical destruction, God maintains that His ways are not our ways. Even allowing His Son to die seems contrary to reason. The use of preaching as the means of communicating the message of the Gospel is also seemingly foolishness to the worldly sophisticated. But this is the means God has selected to spread the message of salvation.

> *For the preaching of the cross is to them that perish foolishness; but unto us which are saved it is the power of God* (I Cor. 1:18).

> *But the natural man receiveth not the things of the Spirit of God: for they are foolishness unto him: neither can he know them, because they are spiritually discerned* (I Cor. 2:14).

> *For my thoughts are not your thoughts, neither are your ways my ways, saith the LORD. For as the heavens are higher than the earth, so are my ways higher than your ways, and my thoughts than your thoughts* (Isa. 55:8, 9).

Christ as the Good Shepherd is self sacrificing. He speaks of Himself in the parable of the Lost Sheep. His love and concern come to the fore as he leaves the ninety-nine which were at hand and goes out to seek the one that was lost. His search takes Him to the full extent of the depravity and degradation of the lost one in order to bring Him back to the fold. The level of rejoicing at finding the one that was lost emphasizes the preciousness of each individual. This is why Jesus says: *"I say unto you, that likewise joy shall be in heaven over one sinner that repented, more than over ninety and nine just persons, which need no repentance"* (Lk. 15:7).

Christ is not only good because He seeks lost ones but He provides to the extent of giving His life for His sheep. A good shepherd will go to great lengths to protect his flock from the attack of wild beasts but this Shepherd became the ultimate sacrifice for His sheep. He gave His very life to procure the safety of His sheep. He says: *"I am the good shepherd: the good shepherd giveth his life for the sheep"* (Jn. 10:11). He went to the cross and suffered a shameful death at the hands of His enemies as payment for the freedom of His sheep. There is now a close bond between the Shepherd and the sheep. *"I am the good shepherd, and know my sheep, and am known of mine"* (Jn. 10:14).

Closely associated with the fact that Christ is the Good Shepherd is the fact that He is the Door. To be precise, He is The Door of the sheep. This again ties in with that which He said before: "I am the way." He is everything to the sheep. The religious leaders in all their wisdom did not understand the things Jesus said to them. They did not understand then and most today display the same problem which was prevalent then: *"This parable spake Jesus unto them: but they understood not what things they were which he spake unto them"* (Jn. 10:6). They sought to lead people to God and did not know the way themselves. They were *"blind leaders of the blind"* (Mt. 15:14).

Along with Himself as care giver Jesus spoke of "hirelings" and also the "porter". Neither of these displays the kind of devotion and care that the Good Shepherd exhibits. At the first sign of trouble the hireling may run and abandon the sheep but the Good Shepherd stays to protect and to comfort the sheep. Their trust in Him keeps them together. He leads them all the way. They know Him and He knows them.

> *Verily, verily, I say unto you, He that entereth not by the door into the sheepfold, but climbeth up some other way, the same is a thief and a robber. But he that entereth in by the door is the shepherd of the*

*sheep. To him the porter openeth; and the sheep hear his voice: and he calleth his own sheep by name, and leadeth them out. And when he putteth forth his own sheep, he goeth before them, and the sheep follow him: for they know his voice. And a stranger will they not follow, but will flee from him: for they know not the voice of strangers* (Jn. 10:1 – 5).

*This parable spake Jesus unto them: but they understood not what things they were which he spake unto them.*

*Then said Jesus unto them again, Verily, verily, I say unto you, I am the door of the sheep.*

*All that ever came before me are thieves and robbers: but the sheep did not hear them. I am the door: by me if any man enter in, he shall be saved, and shall go in and out, and find pasture.*

*The thief cometh not, but for to steal, and to kill, and to destroy: I am come that they might have life, and that they might have it more abundantly. I am the good shepherd: the good shepherd giveth his life for the sheep* (Jn. 10:6 – 11).

Christ made claims that no other religious leader has made and substantiated each with examples from His lifestyle or lived out the claims in incontrovertible ways. The most powerful of His claims is to being life and the resurrection. He allowed Himself to be put to death in the presence of His friends who had not believed before. They were discouraged, dejected, despondent and apathetic after His death. They did not look forward with any measure of anticipation past His death. His resurrection, though, reinvigorated and emboldened them to the point that they were able to withstand the Pharisees and flatly accused them of murdering the Savior. They were a people with a new awareness that could not be quelled even in the face of personal harm and death.

# CHAPTER EIGHT

# LIGHT HAS COME

*Arise, shine; for thy light is come, and the glory of the
LORD is risen upon thee.*

*For, behold, the darkness shall cover the earth,
and gross darkness the people: but the LORD shall
arise upon thee, and his glory shall be seen upon thee*
(Isa 60:1, 2).

*The people that walked in darkness have seen a great
light: they that dwell in the land of the shadow of
death, upon them hath the light shined* (Isa. 9:2).

L ight, as we saw earlier, does not have only to do with
day as opposed to night, neither does it necessarily
have reference to the rays emanating from an artificial
light source nor that which enables one to see. Light has
to do with cognition; the processing and assimilation of
information by the human mind. Information may be
received and stored without a proper understanding of what
it all means; but when understanding comes in then one
sees the "light". Among other definitions of light we have
the following dictionary definitions:

mental insight; understanding.

spiritual illumination or awareness; enlightenment

**Idioms:**

**bring to light,** to discover or reveal: *The excavations brought to light the remnants of an ancient civilization*

**come to light,** to be discovered or revealed: *Some previously undiscovered letters have lately come to light.*[54]

One of the definitions correctly says, "spiritual illumination or awareness; enlightenment." It is in this 'light' the advent of "The Light" will be considered. Early indication of the coming of that 'Light' was given by the prophet Isaiah in the passages quoted above. That Light came through the descendants of the Jews but was for the whole world. More specifically the text says it was to "The people that walked in darkness" and "they that dwell in the land of the shadow of death."

The passage also states, "Darkness shall cover the earth," and that is not the darkness of night although the "works of darkness" are more often performed during the darkness of night. It is into that darkness that the Light of Christ was introduced. Darkness covered the earth although there were all those other religions that we consider early or far eastern. Man was steeped in the darkness of ignorance concerning which Christ brought elucidation. It is for this reason, too, that no other religion can stand in the light of Christianity. Paul, one of the early proponents of Christianity, one of the writers God used to communicate to us the message of the New Testament, expressed this truth in these words:

> *Forasmuch then as we are the offspring of God, we ought not to think that the Godhead is like unto gold, or silver, or stone, graven by art and man's device.*
>
> *And the times of this ignorance God winked at; but now commandeth all men everywhere to repent: because he hath appointed a day, in the which he will*

*judge the world in righteousness by that man whom he hath ordained; whereof he hath given assurance unto all men, in that he hath raised him from the dead* (Acts 17:29 – 31).

Because of Jesus Christ, God no longer overlooks man's ignorance. Such ignorance has been dispelled by that light which entered the realm of earth. Despite the fact that light is come, man persists in his pernicious ways but that will not douse the light. He remains accountable because 'Light has come'.

**Not a new concept:**

The concept of light as enlightenment is not a new one. The Psalmist expresses a well known concept when he makes the following statements:

*For with thee is the fountain of life: in thy light shall we see light* (Ps. 36:9).

*O send out thy light and thy truth: let them lead me; let them bring me unto thy holy hill, and to thy tabernacles* (Ps. 43:3).

*For thou hast delivered my soul from death: wilt not thou deliver my feet from falling, that I may walk before God in the light of the living?* (Ps. 56:13).

*Thy word is a lamp unto my feet, and a light unto my path* (Ps. 119:105).

*The entrance of thy words giveth light; it giveth understanding unto the simple* (Ps. 119:130).

In these passages several aspects of light are mentioned. Each of these is an aspect of the person and mission of Christ. Light is considered as the source of life and truly Christ is the source of all life. It is by walking in that life that the Psalmist sees light for living. Light is also considered as equal to truth. Christ is the way the truth and the life. Both light and truth are to lead to God and His habitation and so is Christ. God's word is an illumination to the feet of the Psalmist so his life is ordered correctly. These words also give light and understanding, and these are part of the mission of Christ. More than that, Jesus is the living Word. John tells us that Jesus was that Word. Jesus is the 'flesh' representation of that Word which was with God in the beginning and which was also God.

> *In the beginning was the Word, and the Word was with God, and the Word was God.*
>
> *And the Word was made flesh, and dwelt among us, (and we beheld his glory, the glory as of the only begotten of the Father,) full of grace and truth* (Jn. 1:1, 14).

Isaiah, who gave us our opening verses, spoke of the Light which would come. He states expressly what the mission and function of that one who would come would be in terms that correlate to what we know of Christ.

> *Behold my servant, whom I uphold; mine elect, in whom my soul delighteth; I have put my spirit upon him: he shall bring forth judgment to the Gentiles.*
>
> *Thus saith God the LORD, he that created the heavens, and stretched them out; he that spread forth the earth, and that which cometh out of it; he that giveth breath unto the people upon it, and spirit to them that walk therein: I the LORD have called thee*

*in righteousness, and will hold thine hand, and will keep thee, and give thee for a covenant of the people, for a light of the Gentiles; to open the blind eyes, to bring out the prisoners from the prison, and them that sit in darkness out of the prison house.*

*I am the LORD: that is my name: and my glory will I not give to another, neither my praise to graven images* (Isa. 42:1, 5 – 8).

The Babylonians, among whom Daniel spent most of his life, understood the concept of light as 'understanding'. They well understood it as having knowledge of things that were not public knowledge. Secrets were not outside the realm of that light. Daniel, too, was familiar with light as having understanding. The queen acknowledged that Daniel's kind of understanding is the kind which resides with the gods – more correctly with God.

*Daniel answered and said, Blessed be the name of God for ever and ever: for wisdom and might are his: and he changeth the times and the seasons: he removeth kings, and setteth up kings: he giveth wisdom unto the wise, and knowledge to them that know understanding: he revealeth the deep and secret things: he knoweth what is in the darkness, and the light dwelleth with him* (Dan. 2:20 – 22).

*Now the queen by reason of the words of the king and his lords came into the banquet house: and the queen spake and said, O king, live for ever: let not thy thoughts trouble thee, nor let thy countenance be changed: there is a man in thy kingdom, in whom is the spirit of the holy gods; and in the days of thy father light and understanding and wisdom, like the wisdom of the gods, was found in him; whom the king Nebuchadnezzar thy father, the king, I say, thy father, made master of the magicians, astrologers, Chaldeans, and soothsayers;* (Dan. 5:10, 11)

The existence of such light, therefore, was well known to the ancients.

## Anticipation of the Light:

That light was anticipated by those who lived at the time of His advent. Zacharias, the father of John the Baptist, was able to muse over the birth of his son in those words:

*And thou, child, shalt be called the prophet of the Highest: for thou shalt go before the face of the Lord to prepare his ways; to give knowledge of salvation unto his people by the remission of their sins, through the tender mercy of our God; whereby the dayspring from on high hath visited us, to give light to them that sit in darkness and in the shadow of death, to guide our feet into the way of peace* (Lk. 1:76 – 79).

Simeon, a man described by the Scriptures as righteous and devout, was expectant of the birth of Jesus Christ. He had received revelation that he would see God's Christ before he died. The Bible describes his sauntering into the Temple and his subsequent reaction to the sight of the baby Jesus like this:

*And, behold, there was a man in Jerusalem, whose name was Simeon; and the same man was just and devout, waiting for the consolation of Israel: and the Holy Ghost was upon him.*

*And it was revealed unto him by the Holy Ghost, that he should not see death, before he had seen the Lord's Christ.*

*And he came by the Spirit into the temple: and when the parents brought in the child Jesus, to do for him after the custom of the law, then took he him up in his arms, and blessed God, and said, "Lord, now lettest thou thy servant depart in peace, according to thy word: for mine eyes have seen thy salvation which thou hast prepared before the face of all people; a light to lighten the Gentiles, and the glory of thy people Israel (Lk. 2:25 – 32).*

## Jesus' acknowledgement of the Light:

Jesus came knowing why He was here. At the onset of His active ministry He made declaration of the fact that He was the Light. Even as He said to the Pharisees on one occasion to 'Search the scriptures, they speak of Me', Jesus acknowledged that the Light spoken of in the Old Testament was He. He had come to fulfill the Scriptures and He was doing so even in this aspect of its proposed 'Light'.

*Now when Jesus had heard that John was cast into prison, he departed into Galilee; and leaving Nazareth, he came and dwelt in Capernaum, which is upon the sea coast, in the borders of Zabulon and Nephthalim: that it might be fulfilled which was spoken by Esaias the prophet, saying, "The land of Zabulon, and the land of Nephthalim, by the way of the sea, beyond Jordan, Galilee of the Gentiles, The people which sat in darkness saw great light; and to them which sat in the region and shadow of death light is sprung up.*

*From that time Jesus began to preach, and to say, Repent: for the kingdom of heaven is at hand* (Mt. 4:12-17).

Jesus started His earthly ministry during the closing days of John the Baptist. John had been the forerunner of Jesus and had performed his mission creditably. Now that his course was complete there was no need for him to languish in the shadows of the ministry of Christ so God graciously allowed him to exit though not in a way that we might have recommended. God's ways are not our ways.

Immediately, Jesus began His ministry with the preaching of repentance towards God. John, too, had preached repentance but in preparation for the coming of the Messiah. Now that the Messiah was here, He had the message of the Kingdom. It was a call to return to God in the only way possible. It was a call to repentance from sin and to a life lived for God. It was a call to come follow Him as He was the way back to God. Fellowship with God was what man lost and Christ came to reestablish that relationship. It was a painful process – for He suffered like we suffer, yet it was a rewarding one – He accomplished His mission and man now has access back to God.

Jesus presented a multifaceted message all with one central theme and purpose. He highlighted the various needs of man in His numerous "I Am's" but all with the only possible solution – Himself. Christ is all that we need. Christ is the only means that God will recognize and so to seek any other means is like being a thief and a robber.

Christ's message was succinctly expressed in these words: *"Then spake Jesus again unto them, saying, I am the light of the world: he that followeth me shall not walk in darkness, but shall have the light of life"* (Jn. 8:12). He was consistent and persistent in declaring the fact that He was light. It is He who would bring true cognition of who God is, what He requires of us and how we can accomplish God's desire for us. Man's concept of God's requirements was obscured by his problem of sin. Man was in a dungeon with no hope of seeing the light of day. Jesus Christ came into that situation to draw man out of his dilemma and gave man something that he did not even realize that he was without. Jesus came to give life and that more abundantly (Jn. 10:10). His sphere of operation was not restricted to his own nationality but encompassed the world. Thus, there is no man outside the sphere of Christ's reach. He is the light of the world.

It is interesting, too, that the light Christ presents is the "light of life". Death and darkness were the lot of unregenerate man. He was under the condemnation of sin which is death and consequently had no real life. Man was like herded cattle going over a precipice to a Godless eternity despite the fact that he had symbolic representation of Christ's sacrificial death in the Pascal lamb. Christ came to free man – that is to redeem him from his debt of sin against God, and to allow him unrestricted access to and fellowship with God.

The prospect of light and life is one that Christ proclaimed. John, too, declared in his introduction of Christ, *In him was life; and the life was the light of men* (Jn. 1:4). Jesus Christ proclaimed *I am the resurrection and the life; he that believeth in me, though he were dead, yet shall he live: and whosoever liveth and believeth in me shall never die* (Jn. 11:25, 26).

**Darkness in man:**

Darkness has been identified as the lack of knowledge or ignorance of man. Man did not know and obviously did not know that he did not know. Consequently he went blissfully about his way faking knowledge that he did not have. Continually the people contended with Christ regarding spiritual and religious matters although Nicodemus one night blurted out: *"Rabbi, we know that thou art a teacher come from God: for no man can do these miracles that thou doest, except God be with him"* (Jn. 3:2). Jesus' response to him proved the point that although they were teachers, they did not know; for Nicodemus did not understand what it meant to be "born again" nor how that was possible for one who had experienced physical birth already.

Christ further explained why there was that darkness over mankind. He said it was because of man's evil heart. Man's dilemma came as a result of his evil heart but was compounded by the fact that he was in the dark and was in the dark about the fact that he was in the dark. His darkness seemingly to him was a form of light. Christ said therefore:

> *The light of the body is the eye: if therefore thine eye be single, thy whole body shall be full of light. But if thine eye be evil, thy whole body shall be full of darkness. If therefore the light that is in thee be darkness, how great is that darkness!* (Mt. 6:22).

John further contends that the light of Christ shone in a darkness which could not fully grasp the significance of His presence. It is not the fault, then, of the light but one that originated with the darkness. Part of the problem of man's darkness was that he preferred the darkness to the light. Man's pleasure in evil caused him to make the choice of remaining in the dark and under condemnation.

> *And the light shineth in darkness; and the darkness comprehended (fully understood) it not.*
> *There was a man sent from God, whose name was John. The same came for a witness, to bear witness of the Light that all men through him might believe. He was not that Light, but was sent to bear witness*

*of that Light. That was the true Light, which lighteth every man that cometh into the world.*

*He was in the world, and the world was made by him, and the world knew him not* (Jn. 1:5 – 10).

*And this is the condemnation, that light is come into the world, and men loved darkness rather than light, because their deeds were evil.*

*For every one that doeth evil hateth the light, neither cometh to the light, lest his deeds should be reproved. But he that doeth truth cometh to the light, that his deeds may be made manifest, that they are wrought in God* (Jn. 3:19 – 21).

Man's hypocrisy was further exposed when Jesus recounted their guarded interest in the light. During the time of John the Baptist the religious leaders showed some fleeting interest in the message that John preached. They were inquisitive enough to enquire of him concerning the one of whom he spake and received adequate information regarding that light. They were satisfied, for a time, to bask in the testimony John had given of the light but their wickedness did not allow their bliss to be long lived.

*Ye sent unto John, and he bare witness unto the truth. But I receive not testimony from man: but these things I say, that ye might be saved. He was a burning and a shining light: and ye were willing for a season to rejoice in his light* (Jn. 5:33 – 35).

There was adequate warning in the teachings of Jesus to warn His hearers of impending danger. They were in danger of losing out because of their unbelief. His messages were clear but their rejection cost them both a proper knowledge of God and their only hope of salvation. Christ emphasized that His presence just then was to bring man to the Father. To reject Him was to reject the Father. They had a desire to accept the Father but not the Son.

> *Jesus cried and said, He that believeth on me, believeth not on me, but on him that sent me. And he that seeth me seeth him that sent me.*
>
> *I am come a light into the world, that whosoever believeth on me should not abide in darkness.*
>
> *And if any man hear my words, and believe not, I judge him not: for I came not to judge the world, but to save the world.*
>
> *He that rejecteth me, and receiveth not my words, hath one that judgeth him: the word that I have spoken, the same shall judge him in the last day* (Jn. 12:44 – 48).

> *Then Jesus said unto them, Yet a little while is the light with you. Walk while ye have the light, lest darkness come upon you: for he that walketh in darkness knoweth not whither he goeth.*
>
> *While ye have light, believe in the light, that ye may be the children of light. These things spake Jesus, and departed, and did hide himself from them* (Jn. 12:35, 36).

### The record of other writers:

We have ample examples and information in the Gospels regarding the contention between the light of Christ and the darkness of the world. Man is not in darkness because he has had no information, but despite the information he has received. Paul, one of the prolific writers of the New Testament, bore witness of that light although, as he declared, he was one born out of due time. He was called to and bore witness of that Light, for He, too, saw that Light in reality. He recounts his experience to King Agrippa in this way:

> *At midday, O king, I saw in the way a light from heaven, above the brightness of the sun, shining round about me and them which journeyed with me.*
>
> *And when we were all fallen to the earth, I heard a voice speaking unto me, and saying in the Hebrew tongue, Saul, Saul, why persecutest thou me? It is hard for thee to kick against the pricks.*
>
> *And I said, 'Who art thou, Lord?' And he said, 'I am Jesus whom thou persecutest. But rise, and stand upon thy feet: for I have appeared unto thee for this purpose, to make thee a minister and a witness both of these things which thou hast seen, and of those things in the which I will appear unto thee; delivering thee from the people, and from the Gentiles, unto whom now I send thee, to open their eyes, and to turn them from darkness to light, and from the power of Satan unto God, that they may receive forgiveness of sins, and inheritance among them which are sanctified by faith that is in me"* (Acts 26:13 – 18).

Paul was not remiss in carrying out the mandate which had been placed on him to bear record of that light. In all the Churches that he established and preached his message was of Christ the Light. To the Jews (of the diaspora in Rome) he wrote:

> *Behold, thou art called a Jew, and restest in the law, and makest thy boast of God and knowest his will, and approvest the things that are more excellent,*

*being instructed out of the law; and art confident that thou thyself art a guide of the blind, a light of them which are in darkness, an instructor of the foolish, a teacher of babes, which hast the form of knowledge and of the truth in the law. Thou therefore which teachest another, teachest thou not thyself? Thou that preachest a man should not steal, dost thou steal?* (Rom. 2:17 – 21).

That Light was the Saviour of the world but it was not without opposition that the message of the Gospel went forth. While there was open opposition to Christ there was equally great opposition to His messengers proclaiming the Gospel. The source of the opposition is exposed as the Devil and Satan. He has affected the Jews to the extent that they did not only reject their Christ, they actively opposed those who would proclaim Christ and exposed their recalcitrance. Satan carries certain titles which exposes his purpose for his actions.

He is the ruler of the darkness of this world. It is not without reason that the world has not accepted Christ. They are evil affected.

*For we wrestle not against flesh and blood, but against principalities, against powers, against the rulers of the darkness of this world, against spiritual wickedness in high places* (Eph. 6:12).

He is also known as the god of this world and the one who prevents mankind from accepting the light. The result is devastating to his kingdom.

*But if our gospel be hid, it is hid to them that are lost: in whom the god of this world hath blinded the minds of them which believe not, lest the light of the glorious gospel of Christ, who is the image of God, should shine unto them.*

*For we preach not ourselves, but Christ Jesus the Lord; and ourselves your servants for Jesus' sake.*

*For God, who commanded the light to shine out of darkness, hath shined in our hearts, to give the light of the knowledge of the glory of God in the face of Jesus Christ* (II Cor. 4:3 – 6).

Paul had further instructions to others of the Churches he wrote to. To the Ephesians and Thessalonians he wrote:

*For ye were sometimes darkness, but now are ye light in the Lord: walk as children of light:*

*But all things that are reproved are made manifest by the light: for whatsoever doth make manifest is light.*

*Wherefore he saith, Awake thou that sleepest, and arise from the dead, and Christ shall give thee light* (Eph. 5:8, 13 - 14).

*Ye are all the children of light, and the children of the day: we are not of the night, nor of darkness* (I Thess. 5:5).

Peter chimes in with more assurance to the Gentiles regarding their new position in Christ. They are no longer children of the dark but are now children of the light. In this new relationship there should be a life change which would reflect that new relationship.

*But ye are a chosen generation, a royal priesthood, an holy nation, a peculiar people; that ye should show forth the praises of him who hath called you out of darkness into his marvellous light: which in time past were not a people, but are now the people of God: which had not obtained mercy, but now have obtained mercy* (I Pet. 2:9, 10).

*We have also a more sure word of prophecy; whereunto ye do well that ye take heed, as unto a light that shineth in a dark place, until the day dawn, and the day star arise in your hearts: knowing this first, that no prophecy of the scripture is of any private interpretation. For the prophecy came not in old time by the will of man: but holy men of God spake as they were moved by the Holy Ghost* (II Pet. 1:19 – 21).

John also wrote regarding one's relationship with the Light. Having established fellowship with Christ one cannot continue in one's previous walk as in the dark. One's actions reflect the veracity of one's professed relationship to Christ.

*If we say that we have fellowship with him, and walk in darkness, we lie, and do not the truth: but if we walk in the light, as he is in the light, we have fellowship one with another, and the blood of Jesus Christ his Son cleanseth us from all sin* (I Jn. 1:6, 7).

*Again, a new commandment I write unto you, which thing is true in him and in you: because the darkness is past, and the true light now shineth.*

*He that saith he is in the light, and hateth his brother, is in darkness even until now.*

*He that loveth his brother abideth in the light, and there is none occasion of stumbling in him.*

*But he that hateth his brother is in darkness, and walketh in darkness, and knoweth not whither he goeth, because that darkness hath blinded his eyes* (I Jn. 2:8- 11).

The light will reach its effulgence in the new heaven and new earth. God's desire is that we share such light with Him.

*And the city had no need of the sun, neither of the moon, to shine in it: for the glory of God did lighten it, and the Lamb is the light thereof.*

*And the nations of them which are saved shall walk in the light of it: and the kings of the earth do bring their glory and honour into it* (Rev. 21:23 – 24)

*And there shall be no night there; and they need no candle, neither light of the sun; for the Lord God giveth them light: and they shall reign for ever and ever* (Rev. 22:5).

# CHAPTER NINE

# YOU MUST BE BORN AGAIN

In conversation with one of the rulers of the Jews Jesus made this most profound statement – "You must be born again." Three times Jesus jarred the consciousness of Nicodemus with the absolute necessity of the rebirth. It is something necessary in order to see the kingdom of God and it is also necessary to enter the kingdom of God. To see again carries the idea of mental perception but it also carries the connotation of experiencing. This heavenly experience, although simple, is intricately interwoven with one's mental disposition to do so as well as a heart's desire to participate in it. One cannot experience the kingdom of God simply with the fleeting interest of a spectator. One must be moved into the kingdom in full participation in order to enter.

The kingdom of Heaven is different from the kingdom of the earth. Physical birth is necessary in order to enter the realm of the earth. Likewise a birth into the kingdom of heaven is necessary if one is to experience it. Unlike the kingdom of the earth the process is different. Jesus pointed out that a physical birth is necessary for life on earth, but a spiritual birth is necessary for life in the kingdom of God. *"That which is born of the flesh is flesh; and that which is born of the spirit is spirit"* (Jn. 3:6). It is that life that man lost when he sinned in the Garden of Eden.

Man's dilemma in Eden did not only result in physical death, the process of which started immediately and was fulfilled individually hundreds of years later when each in turn left the realm of this earth. Man also lost fellowship and communication with God. God had not made man to be estranged from Him so with due consideration for man's inability to restore that lost relationship, God had to take the initiative to restore it. It was God who came seeking man when He asked, "Adam, where art thou?" It was God who made the provision of an animal sacrifice which was substitutionary, symbolical and typical of what was necessary to restore man.

Man's sin exposed his nakedness. That was both physical and spiritual. In order to redress his physical situation man sewed fig leaves together. That was woefully inadequate for his physical need and most definitely could not provide for his spiritual loss. The leaves represented man's effort to provide for his situation. From then man realized that his efforts were inadequate and unacceptable. Man could not appease God for the destruction that had entered the relationship between God and man. Sin had entered and man knew that he had lost out. What he did not know then was that restoration was possible only through an innocent substitute whose blood had to be shed. This we are made painfully aware of in the New Testament in the words of the writer of Hebrews: "*Without the shedding of blood*, (there) *is no remission*" (Heb. 9:22).

Although the Bible does not say in so many words, that the animal was the symbolic substitution for man's Redeemer, yet we understand it as such as we see God's more permanent provision for man's physical need. Adam's effort to cover his nakedness was inadequate. God provided animal skin for clothing instead of Adam's leaves. It is obvious, though, that the skin was not obtained without the sacrifice of the animal. God's requirement has remained consistent throughout the Bible – blood for blood.

The story continues to play out in the lives of the first two sons of Adam and Eve. In the process of time each one brought an offering to God. Abel brought of the flocks that he tended while Cain brought of the fruit that he had produced in his garden. The offering of Abel was accepted while that of Cain was rejected. An important distinction between the two offerings was the blood. One can reasonably assume that these boys brought offerings in the first place because of custom. They either had been instructed to do so or had observed the lifestyle of their parents. It could be, too, that it was a result of both.

It must be noted that God made this requirement painstakingly clear to the children of Israel before they left Egypt. The offering of the Pascal Lamb was symbolic of the offering which the Lamb of God would offer for the sins of the world. It was the presence of the blood upon the doorposts which allowed the death angel to pass over their houses. The formation of the blood on the posts, too, was symbolic. It represented Christ's sacrifice on the cross. Since Christ's sacrifice, there is no need for another for this is God's provision for the sins of mankind.

*But Christ being come an high priest of good things to come, by a greater and more perfect tabernacle, not made with hands, that is to say, not of this building; neither by the blood of goats and calves, but by his own blood he entered in once into the holy place, having obtained eternal redemption for us.*

*For if the blood of bulls and of goats, and the ashes of an heifer sprinkling the unclean, sanctifieth to the purifying of the flesh: how much more shall the blood of Christ, who through the eternal Spirit offered himself without spot to God, purge your conscience from dead works to serve the living God?*

*And for this cause he is the mediator of the New Testament that by means of death, for the redemption of the transgressions that were under the first testament, they which are called might receive the promise of eternal inheritance. For where a testament is, there must also of necessity be the death of the testator. For a testament is of force after men are dead: otherwise it is of no strength at all while the testator liveth.*

*Whereupon neither the first testament was dedicated without blood* (Heb. 9:11 – 14).

Jesus also pointed out that process and provision to Nicodemus in their discourse when He said: *"And as Moses lifted up the serpent in the wilderness, even so must the Son of man be lifted up: that whosoever believeth in him should not perish, but have eternal life"* (Jn. 3:14, 15). Moses' raising the brass snake on a stick in the wilderness for the healing of the children of Israel who had been snake bitten was symbolic of the crucifixion of Christ. Even so it was necessary for Christ to die such a death in order that man might be restored to God. In his restored condition man cannot be subject to death, thus the provision is also for eternal life. Be reminded that only Christ is The Life.

Because that is the only acceptable provision before God, we "must be born again." The message was not only for Nicodemus but for all mankind. Each one is subject to the death sentence of sin through Adam and each one is required to be born again if he is to 'see' and enter the kingdom of God.

**Man can do nothing to save himself:**

In some small way, it has been noted that man was unable to find his way out of his dilemma. But the situation was impossible for man. It would necessitate man's death for each sin that he committed for "*the wages of sin is death*" (Rom. 6:23). As it is, man only has one life and to have paid for one sin would have left man indebted for every other sin that he had committed. Another possibility was that man could only have sinned once. Swift execution of punishment would have brought about his demise. The purpose of man – to have fellowship with God – would have been impossible. The solution necessitated both payment for the wrong and a means of restoring the broken relationship.

As has been seen, not only was it necessary to pay for sin, it was necessary that the broken fellowship be restored. Man had the ability to do neither. Jesus said to Nicodemus, "*That which is born of the flesh is flesh; and that which is born of the spirit is spirit.*" Man did not have the ability to bring about physical or spiritual birth. Man today is seeking some means of reproducing physical life but has not succeeded. Man has formulated a cloning process but there are two problems that readily come to mind. He has to use material from the original to bring about his creation. That means that the new entity is still affected by the old for they are one and the same. The next impossibility is to make a spirit man. It is one's spirit which man used to communicate with God. Having lost the ability to communicate, man is without the ability to reach out to God. He does not even have the desire to find God. God's word tells us, *As it is written, 'There is none righteous, no, not one: there is none that understandeth, there is none that seeketh after God. They are all gone out of the way, they are together become unprofitable; there is none that doeth good, no, not one'* (Rom. 3:10 – 12).

Was it not possible that man could earn his way into that relationship with God? No! Man possesses a priceless, part of himself which cannot be redeemed with money or its equivalent in work. Even the thought of work presents additional problems which are irreconcilable with the program of God. For one thing God asks the question: "*For what is a man profited, if he shall gain the whole world, and lose his own soul? Or what shall a man give in exchange for his soul?"* (Mt. 16:26). It is obvious that the wealth of the whole world is not comparable to the value of one soul before God. One can give nothing in exchange either, because one does not have enough to give.

The purchase price of man, though prohibitive to man, was possible for God. That is why only He could make provision. Only holy blood could pay the price of every one of man's sins.

> *And if ye call on the Father, who without respect of persons judgeth according to every man's work, pass the time of your sojourning here in fear: forasmuch as ye know that ye were not redeemed with corruptible things, as silver and gold, from your vain conversation received by tradition from your fathers; but with the precious blood of Christ, as of a lamb without blemish and without spot...* (I Pet. 1:17 – 19).

If man were able to pay for his transgressions against God, man would have had another problem. He would have been consumed with pride which is what brought Lucifer to become the Devil. God gave us the rationale behind that impossible task. If man were able to work his way out of his situation, he would have been able to boast but before God that would be meaningless. So the Scriptures gave us the example of Abraham:

> *What shall we say then that Abraham our father, as pertaining to the flesh, hath found? For if Abraham were justified by works, he hath whereof to glory; but not before God. For what saith the scripture? Abraham believed God, and it was counted unto him for righteousness.*

*Now to him that worketh is the reward not reckoned of grace, but of debt. But to him that worketh not, but believeth on him that justifieth the ungodly, his faith is counted for righteousness* (Rom. 4:1 – 4).

Abraham, called the father of faith, had to act on the promises which had been made to him by God. One realizes the promises were not a result of Abraham's efforts or else Abraham would have been able to claim some of the praise for his efforts. It was all as a result of his exercising faith in God who promised which afforded him the blessings. God had promised and could not go back on His word. God was well able so, regardless of circumstances or physical conditions, God fulfilled His word. As a matter of fact God waited until any human effort on Abraham's part was no longer possible to fulfill his promises so that there would be no claim to human effort.

Another difficulty which God clarified was the difference between a gift and wages. To one who has exerted effort or labor one does not offer a gift but wages. Gifts flow from the goodness of the heart of the giver but work demands compensation. Compensations are not termed gifts. What Abraham received was a gift because it was not a result of his effort but the fulfillment of promises made to him by God.

Because of some misconceptions regarding man's soul it is necessary to make some observations here. One is well aware that in speech or writing there are figures of speech which serve to color language to make it more understandable or even attractive. One such is a synecdoche. One example is 'the arm of flesh' for man's strength or human effort. Similarly soul is sometimes used to refer to the whole person. But that is not always so. There are verses of scripture which bear out the fact that man is not only referred to as being a soul but also as having a soul. Hence the question: "What shall a man give in exchange for his soul?" Special note must be taken that the personal, possessive pronoun "his" is used before soul. It is obvious that this is a possession of man and not simply man.

Not only does man possess his soul but the Scriptures tell us that God possesses the soul of man and calls him into account for it. To ask "What shall a man give in exchange for his soul?" also implies accountability. It also suggests that man may erroneously batter his soul for something of much less value. The prophet Job recognizes the activity of God in the management of the soul. Things happen which should goad one in the direction of God. So he says, "*Who knoweth not in all these that the hand of the LORD hath wrought this? In whose hand is the soul of every living thing, and the breath of all mankind*" (Job 12:9).

Another Scripture shows that the soul of man is a part of him just as his heart. Reference is made to both in the same breath and joined by a coordinating conjunction. *And the king stood in his place, and made a covenant before the LORD, to walk after the LORD, and to keep his commandments, and his testimonies, and his statutes, with all his heart, and with all his soul, to perform the words of the covenant which are written in this book* (II Chr. 34:31). Lest one should think that the king was not knowledgeable enough we note Jesus, the creator, responding to the young ruler in these words, *"Jesus said unto him, Thou shalt love the Lord thy God with all thy heart, and with all thy soul, and with all thy mind"* (Mt. 22:37). If anyone would know of the parts of man, Jesus should. He delineates man as having heart and soul and mind. An austere warning from Christ should seal the question beyond doubt: *"And fear not them which kill the body, but are not able to kill the soul: but rather fear him which is able to destroy both soul and body in hell"* (Mt. 10:28).

The soul and body could perish separately and by different means.

Jesus further uses this dissection with reference to Himself. As He faced the prospect of the cross, in His humanity, Jesus suffered with apprehension. The premonition of the suffering of the cross caused Him to sweat great drops of blood. He enjoined his disciples in these words, *"My soul is exceeding sorrowful, even unto death: tarry ye here, and watch with me"* (Mt. 26:38). He spoke of "His soul" as being sorrowful.

It is also very significant that the soul can be saved. Although the body can die and will die, the soul can be saved. The Psalmist extols the Word of God recognizing its ability to turn the soul away from its wicked ways and to turn it to God. He says: *"The law of the LORD is perfect, converting the soul: the testimony of the LORD is sure, making wise the simple"* (Ps. 19:7). The converted soul is going to inhabit a renewed body in the resurrection.

### There is no other way to enter heaven:

It is a common phenomenon to find people thinking that there are various ways to enter heaven. Jesus, in His statement of exclusivity, made it clear that He was the only way. Without going through the details of that verse again one must emphasize that there is no other way. One saw, too, that man is incapable of satisfying God's just demand in recompense for sin. The soul that sins, it shall die. Neither Jesus nor his disciples preached any other means of achieving salvation or eternal life. Other religions do not make it.

A rich young ruler came to Jesus once with the question, *"Good Master, what good thing shall I do that I may have eternal life?"* Jesus accommodatingly and condescendingly responded that, *"...if thou wilt have life keep the commandments."* Gleefully, the young ruler responded that he had kept all from his youth. Jesus did not contradict him but tactfully put his finger on one of the major problems that not only the young ruler but mankind generally trusts in – riches. Two things became very apparent in the reaction of the young ruler – his love and greed for riches. These are very common problems for those who would enter heaven. Their riches will not enable them but may prevent rich men from eternal life. Although, as Jesus pointed out to His disciples, it is not impossible, but not too many rich are called. The rich man in the story of the rich man and Lazarus found that out too late.

Going back to the rich young ruler's question, "What good thing...?" it must be observed that there are no good people and so there are consequently no good things which could be done. The Scriptures conclude that man's disposition is not favorable for salvation.

> *What then? Are we better than they? No, in no wise: for we have before proved both Jews and Gentiles, that they are all under sin; as it is written, 'There is none righteous, no, not one: there is none that understandeth, there is none that seeketh after God. They are all gone out of the way, they are together become unprofitable; there is none that doeth good, no, not one'* (Rom. 3:9 – 12).

The rich man realized, too, that the deeds of the Law offered no respite from the guilt of sin. While one realizes the extent of sin through the Law, keeping the Law does not afford redemption from sin. So God says:

> *Therefore by the deeds of the law there shall no flesh be justified in his sight: for by the law is the knowledge of sin.*

*But now the righteousness of God without the law is manifested, being witnessed by the law and the prophets; even the righteousness of God which is by faith of Jesus Christ unto all and upon all them that believe: for there is no difference. For all have sinned, and come short of the glory of God; Being justified freely by his grace through the redemption that is in Christ Jesus: whom God hath set forth to be a propitiation through faith in his blood, to declare his righteousness for the remission of sins that are past, through the forbearance of God; to declare, I say, at this time his righteousness: that he might be just, and the justifier of him which believeth in Jesus.*

*Where is boasting then? It is excluded. By what law? Of works? Nay: but by the law of faith* (Rom. 3:20 – 27).

*Now to him that worketh is the reward not reckoned of grace, but of debt. But to him that worketh not, but believeth on him that justifieth the ungodly, his faith is counted for righteousness* (Rom. 4:4).

*For the wages of sin is death; but the gift of God is eternal life through Jesus Christ our Lord* (Rom. 6:23).

God's method is unbiased and without prejudice.

The disciples, too, preached Christ as the way to God and eternal life. From the day of Pentecost, when the disciples began to preach, Christ was presented. In answer to the Pharisees who challenged their authority to preach and heal the disciples responded:

*Be it known unto you all, and to all the people of Israel, that by the name of Jesus Christ of Nazareth, whom ye crucified, whom God raised from the dead, even by him doth this man stand here before you whole.*

*This is the stone which was set at nought of you builders, which is become the head of the corner.*

*Neither is there salvation in any other: for there is none other name under heaven given among men, whereby we must be saved* (Acts 4:10 – 12).

## Christ is God's only provision:

Since man was incapable of doing anything about his spiritual condition, God took the initiative to provide man with a way of escape. God, from the beginning, intimated that such provision was forthcoming. In the Old Testament, several symbols and types were used to point to the means that God would provide for sin. Man's efforts were continually frowned upon and Israel was presented as God's showpiece of His grace. Israel did not live up to expectations but that did not thwart God's plans for mankind. He is The Almighty God.

> *For thus saith the LORD that created the heavens; God himself that formed the earth and made it; he hath established it, he created it not in vain, he formed it to be inhabited: I am the LORD; and there is none else.*
>
> *I have not spoken in secret, in a dark place of the earth: I said not unto the seed of Jacob, Seek ye me in vain: I the LORD speak righteousness, I declare things that are right. Assemble yourselves and come; draw near together, ye that are escaped of the nations: they have no knowledge that set up the wood of their graven image, and pray unto a god that cannot save.*

*Tell ye, and bring them near; yea, let them take counsel together: who hath declared this from ancient time? Who hath told it from that time? Have not I the LORD? And there is no God else beside me; a just God and a Saviour; there is none beside me.*

*Look unto me, and be ye saved, all the ends of the earth: for I am God, and there is none else. I have sworn by myself, the word is gone out of my mouth in righteousness, and shall not return, That unto me every knee shall bow, every tongue shall swear.*

*Surely, shall one say, in the LORD have I righteousness and strength: even to him shall men come; and all that are incensed against him shall be ashamed.*

*In the LORD shall all the seed of Israel be justified, and shall glory* (Isa. 45:18 - 25).

God prefigured the death of Jesus Christ to the children of Israel after they had left Egypt and before they entered the promised land. Because of their rebellion God had sent snakes among them to destroy them. As a remedy for their poisonous infections Moses was commanded to make a brazen serpent and put it up on a pole. All that was necessary then was for the Israelites to look to the serpent and live. In the New Testament, God points to that experience in the wilderness as a type of what would happen to Christ and the efficacy of that sacrifice.

*And as Moses lifted up the serpent in the wilderness, even so must the Son of man be lifted up: that whosoever believeth in him should not perish, but have eternal life.*

*For God so loved the world, that he gave his only begotten Son, that whosoever believeth in him should not perish, but have everlasting life* (Jn. 3:14 – 16).

The whole purpose of Christ's coming was to save. *For the Son of man is come to seek and to save that which was lost.* (Lk. 19:10) God's plan is further elucidated in the following verses:

*For God sent not his Son into the world to condemn the world; but that the world through him might be saved.*

*He that believeth on him is not condemned: but he that believeth not is condemned already, because he hath not believed in the name of the only begotten Son of God.*

*And this is the condemnation, that light is come into the world, and men loved darkness rather than light, because their deeds were evil.*

*He that believeth on the Son hath everlasting life: and he that believeth not the Son shall not see life; but the wrath of God abideth on him* (Jn. 3:17 – 19, 36).

That the provision of God is adequate to solve the problem between God and man, God presents the following consolation:

*Being justified freely by his grace through the redemption that is in Christ Jesus: Whom God hath set forth to be a propitiation through faith in his blood, to declare his righteousness for the remission of sins that are past, through the forbearance of God; To declare, I say, at this time his righteousness: that he might be just, and the justifier of him which believeth in Jesus* (Rom. 3:24 – 26).

*Therefore being justified by faith, we have peace with God through our Lord Jesus Christ: by whom also we have access by faith into this grace wherein we stand, and rejoice in hope of the glory of God* (Rom. 5:1, 2).

*There is therefore now no condemnation to them which are in Christ Jesus, who walk not after the flesh, but after the Spirit.*

*For the law of the Spirit of life in Christ Jesus hath made me free from the law of sin and death.*

*For what the law could not do, in that it was weak through the flesh, God sending his own Son in the likeness of sinful flesh, and for sin, condemned sin in the flesh: that the righteousness of the law might be fulfilled in us, who walk not after the flesh, but after the Spirit* (Rom. 8:1 – 4).

*And he is the propitiation for our sins: and not for ours only, but also for the sins of the whole world* (I Jn. 2:2).

*Herein is love, not that we loved God, but that he loved us, and sent his Son to be the propitiation for our sins* (I Jn. 4:10).

Having established the fact that there is no other way, and that Jesus Christ is the only provision which would satisfy God's just demand for the remission of sin, the Bible goes on to list, though not exhaustively, some definite actions which man engages in which, apart from original sin, definitely excludes man from God's presence. Man continues to pile up condemnation against himself even in the face of all that God has provided. His works are listed:

*Know ye not that the unrighteous shall not inherit the kingdom of God? Be not deceived: neither fornicators, nor idolaters, nor adulterers, nor effeminate, nor abusers of themselves with mankind, nor thieves, nor covetous, nor drunkards, nor revilers, nor extortioners, shall inherit the kingdom of God* (I Cor. 6:9, 10).

*Now the works of the flesh are manifest, which are these; Adultery, fornication, uncleanness, lasciviousness, idolatry, witchcraft, hatred, variance, emulations, wrath, strife, seditions, heresies, envyings, murders, drunkenness, revellings, and such like: of the which I tell you before, as I have also told you in time past, that they which do such things shall not inherit the kingdom of God* (Gal. 5:19 – 21).

*But the fearful, and unbelieving, and the abominable, and murderers, and whoremongers, and sorcerers, and idolaters, and all liars, shall have their part in the lake which burneth with fire and brimstone: which is the second death* (Rev. 21:8).

**The reality of hell:**

The concept of hell is one that has been ridiculed by many. Some think that hell is here on earth while others think that it is simply the grave. Some references in the Bible seem to picture the place outside of Jerusalem where garbage was disposed of and burned. Each of these has some relevance depending on the context in which it is used. But the Bible speaks of a specific place called hell which is the final abode of the unrighteous.

The reality of hell is heightened when one considers the major proponent of that place. Jesus Christ speaks most and very specifically about the place called hell. It is a place where no pleasantries abound.

*But I say unto you, That whosoever is angry with his brother without a cause shall be in danger of the judgment: and whosoever shall say to his brother, Raca, shall be in danger of the council: but whosoever shall say, Thou fool, shall be in danger of hell fire.*

> *And if thy right eye offend thee, pluck it out, and cast it from thee: for it is profitable for thee that one of thy members should perish, and not that thy whole body should be cast into hell.*
>
> *And if thy right hand offend thee, cut it off, and cast it from thee: for it is profitable for thee that one of thy members should perish, and not that thy whole body should be cast into hell* (Mt. 5:22, 29 – 30).

The thought of such a place should create a particular type of fear within one.

> *And fear not them which kill the body, but are not able to kill the soul: but rather fear him which is able to destroy both soul and body in hell* (Mt. 10:28).

Whole cities seem to be affected by the consequence of rejecting Christ.

> *And thou, Capernaum, which art exalted unto heaven, shalt be brought down to hell: for if the mighty works, which have been done in thee, had been done in Sodom, it would have remained until this day* (Mt. 11:23).

It is in opposition to the work of God:

> *And I say also unto thee, 'That thou art Peter, and upon this rock I will build my church; and the gates of hell shall not prevail against it'* Mt. (16:18).

It is an eternal fire:

> *Wherefore if they hand or thy foot offend thee, cut them off, and cast them from thee: it is better for thee*

*to enter into life halt or maimed, rather than having two hands or two feet to be cast into everlasting fire (Mt. 18:8).*

Being a member of the Jewish religion will not save. In some cases this may be the hindrance. Other religions will have the same effect on persons.

*Woe unto you, scribes and Pharisees, hypocrites! For ye compass sea and land to make one proselyte, and when he is made, ye make him twofold more the child of hell than yourselves.*

*Ye serpents, ye generation of vipers, how can ye escape the damnation of hell?* (Mt. 23:15, 33)

## Instead of consuming, hell fire preserves:

*And if thy hand offend thee, cut it off: it is better for thee to enter into life maimed, than having two hands to go into hell, into the fire that never shall be quenched: where their worm dieth not, and the fire is not quenched.*

*For every one shall be salted with fire, and every sacrifice shall be salted with salt* (Mk. 9:43 – 44, 49).

## It is a place of torment:

*And in hell he lift up his eyes, being in torments, and seeth Abraham afar off, and Lazarus in his bosom* (Lk 16:23).

Hell is a holding place for outrageously outlandish demons (no pun intended):

*For if God spared not the angels that sinned, but cast them down to hell, and delivered them into chains of darkness, to be reserved unto judgment;* (II Pet 2:4)

The tongue is a member of the body with great capabilities. One of the deadliest potentials is the ability to cause persons to go to hell.

*And the tongue is a fire, a world of iniquity: so is the tongue among our members, that it defileth the whole body, and setteth on fire the course of nature; and it is set on fire of hell* (James 3:6).

Christ says that He is in possession of the keys of hell. He should know if there is a hell. He has the keys.

*I am he that liveth, and was dead; and, behold, I am alive for evermore, Amen; and have the keys of hell and of death* (Rev. 1:18).

Death and hell are partners. Death closes the door to any opportunity to escape hell.

*And I looked, and behold a pale horse: and his name that sat on him was Death, and Hell followed with him. And power was given unto them over the fourth part of the earth, to kill with sword, and with hunger, and with death, and with the beasts of the earth* (Rev. 6:8).

Nothing can prevent deserving ones from going to hell. Death by drowning cannot; cremation with the ashes scattered over the sea cannot; death by fire cannot preclude one. No form of death will shield anyone from coming forth to face the judgment. Hell, regardless of your perception of what it is, will not keep anyone away from the judgment and final place of abode of the wicked. Death and hell themselves will be cast into that final place of destruction. Everyone who does not have the life offered by Christ will be an occupant of the lake of fire.

> *And the sea gave up the dead which were in it; and death and hell delivered up the dead which were in them: and they were judged every man according to their works.*
>
> *And death and hell were cast into the lake of fire. This is the second death.*
>
> *And whosoever was not found written in the book of life was cast into the lake of fire* (Rev. 20:13 – 15).

Considering the magnitude of God's provision no one will be allowed to proffer any other way to God. To reject God's offer in favor of some man-made measure has devastating consequences. The imperative remains, "You must be born again.

# CHAPTER TEN

# THE ETERNAL HOPE

Tolerance is a bridle; a gag to silence the voice of the Gospel message. The Gospel is not all inclusive of those who are religious; but is a light to draw sinners to God. To escape the dreadfulness of hell:

The final end of life on earth should be of vital importance to any reasonably concerned person. But sad to say, some would rather leave such an important matter to chance, to time, to oblivion, and to misconception. To some, one should try various possibilities and hope that in the final analysis the right choice would have been made. As a matter of fact, we live in a time where the power of choice is exalted. This seems to be the inalienable right of each one regardless of reason or consequences. Choice is a powerful tool but it must operate within the realm of adequate information to be of value. Time is also a very precious commodity that one often thinks he has an ample supply of. While this is the hope of each one, reality would readily advise that one has no control over time. Opportunity comes and goes, but time keeps moving on until suddenly it is no more. Oblivion rides on both time and choice until time decides to quit then choice has no power any more. When reality comes in, then there is realization that nothing can be done about one's situation.

The rich man, in the story of Lazarus and the rich man, had a very rude awakening but that was in hell. He was advised by Abraham to remember – something he had not had time for. His reflections brought only regrets; and his desires, borne out of his power of choice, were ineffective. He desired water but that was not forthcoming. He desired the services of Lazarus but that was denied. He desired that his brothers be warned not to squander their opportunities like he had done, but that was futile. He still had a last ditch effort desiring that one come from the dead and warn his brothers, but that was ridiculed. Don't think it strange that a loving God would ridicule such a serious request. He would.

> *How long, ye simple ones, will ye love simplicity? And the scorners delight in their scorning, and fools hate knowledge?*
>
> *Turn you at my reproof: behold, I will pour out my spirit unto you, I will make known my words unto you.*
>
> *Because I have called, and ye refused; I have stretched out my hand, and no man regarded; but ye have set at nought all my counsel, and would none of my reproof: I also will laugh at your calamity; I will mock when your fear cometh; when your fear cometh as desolation, and your destruction cometh as a whirlwind; when distress and anguish cometh upon you.*
>
> *Then shall they call upon me, but I will not answer; they shall seek me early, but they shall not find me: for that they hated knowledge, and did not choose the fear of the LORD: they would none of my counsel: they despised all my reproof. Therefore shall they eat of the fruit of their own way, and be filled with their own devices* (Prov. 1:22 – 31) .

You were heard. No! This is not insensitivity; this is not a lack of compassion. Compassion is taking your place on a cursed cross; suffering shame and disgrace in your place, and making it possible that you go free. Insensitivity is looking such love and compassion in the face and rejecting it choosing instead to ignore it, wait for a time convenient to your agenda or even seeking an alternative when such elaborate preparation has been made for you.

The rich man prayed that a message be sent from the great beyond to warn his brothers not to come to that place of torment. His request was not granted as he wished, but it was granted. You have the record of his wish and his testimony of the conditions there. Wisdom dictates that you not seek to experience for yourself first before you heed his warning; for if you do it would be just as late for you as it was for him. Then your fortune cannot be turned around. *"…it is appointed unto men once to die and after this the judgment…"* You can do something about it now.

> *Wherefore (as the Holy Ghost saith, Today if ye will hear his voice, Harden not your hearts, as in the provocation, in the day of temptation in the wilderness: When your fathers tempted me, proved me, and saw my works forty years. Wherefore I was grieved with that generation, and said, 'They do always err in their heart; and they have not known my ways'. So I sware in my wrath, 'They shall not enter into my rest.')*
>
> *Take heed, brethren, lest there be in any of you an evil heart of unbelief, in departing from the living God* (Heb. 3:7 – 12).

Can you honestly at this point claim ignorance as an excuse for not accepting Christ as the only way? Any misconception on your part is willful ignorance. All that is required is faith in what Christ has done. No! Faith is not blind acceptance. Instead, this kind of faith is believing, in the light of the available information, in the ability of Christ, adequately demonstrated in His raising others before Him from the dead and rising, himself, from the dead. Believing that He can and will fulfill His promises. He can and He will. Put your trust and confidence in Him now and you can be among those who wait for His return.

## To be where God is:

The eternal hope of the Christian is to be with God where he is. It is the promise of Christ to His disciples before He left them. That promise was not only to the twelve but to all who would accept Him and live for Him. Christ gave that assurance in these words:

> *Let not your heart be troubled: ye believe in God, believe also in me. In my Father's house are many mansions: if it were not so, I would have told you. I go to prepare a place for you. And if I go and prepare a place for you, I will come again, and receive you unto myself; that where I am, there ye may be also* (Jn. 14:1 – 3).

As He prayed for His followers in John seventeen Christ said to the Father, *Neither pray I for these alone, but for them also which shall believe on me through their word; that they all may be one; as thou, Father, art in me, and I in thee, that they also may be one in us: that the world may believe that thou hast sent me* (Jn. 17:20, 21). All who would come to Him as a result of the preaching of the disciples are included in the prayer that Christ made.

Christ further gave the assurance that, though death may come between the time He leaves and the time He returns, that would not prevent the reunion and continuous future fellowship of those who are His. One has this assurance:

> *All that the Father giveth me shall come to me; and him that cometh to me I will in no wise cast out.*
>
> *And this is the Father's will which hath sent me, that of all which he hath given me I should lose nothing, but should raise it up again at the last day.*
>
> *And this is the will of him that sent me, that every one which seeth the Son, and believeth on him, may have everlasting life: and I will raise him up at the last day.*
>
> *No man can come to me, except the Father which hath sent me draw him: and I will raise him up at the last day.*
>
> *Whoso eateth my flesh, and drinketh my blood, hath eternal life; and I will raise him up at the last day* (Jn. 6:37, 39, 40, 44, 54). (Underline mine).

The Apostle Paul preached that eternal hope to all of the Churches where he went. His personal expectation was to be with the Lord. As he faced the end of his mission on earth he said to the Philippians: *"For I am in a strait betwixt two, having a desire to depart, and to be with Christ; which is far better:"* (Phil. 1:23). His desire was to be with the Lord, but for the time it was more beneficial for the Church that he remained. To the other Churches he said:

> *Therefore we are always confident, knowing that, whilst we are at home in the body, we are absent from the Lord. (For we walk by faith, not by sight.) We are confident, I say, and willing rather to be absent from the body, and to be present with the Lord. Wherefore we labour, that, whether present or absent, we may be accepted of him* (II Cor. 5:6 – 9).

*Blessed be the God and Father of our Lord Jesus Christ, who hath blessed us with all spiritual blessings in heavenly places in Christ: according as he hath chosen us in him before the foundation of the world, that we should be holy and without blame before him in love: having predestinated us unto the adoption of children by Jesus Christ to himself, according to the good pleasure of his will, to the praise of the glory of his grace, wherein he hath made us accepted in the beloved.*

*In whom we have redemption through his blood, the forgiveness of sins, according to the riches of his grace; wherein he hath abounded toward us in all wisdom and prudence; having made known unto us the mystery of his will, according to his good pleasure which he hath purposed in himself: that in the dispensation of the fullness of times he might gather together in one all things in Christ, both which are in heaven, and which are on earth; even in him in whom also we have obtained an inheritance, being predestinated according to the purpose of him who worketh all things after the counsel of his own will: that we should be to the praise of his glory, who first trusted in Christ.*

*In whom ye also trusted, after that ye heard the word of truth, the gospel of your salvation: in whom also after that ye believed, ye were sealed with that Holy Spirit of promise, which is the earnest (or down payment) of our inheritance until the redemption of the purchased possession, unto the praise of his glory* (Eph 1:3 – 14).

*But I would not have you to be ignorant, brethren, concerning them which are asleep, that ye sorrow not, even as others which have no hope. For if we believe that Jesus died and rose again, even so them also which sleep(are dead) in Jesus will God bring with him.*

*For this we say unto you by the word of the Lord, that we which are alive and remain unto the coming of the Lord shall not prevent them which are asleep.*

*For the Lord himself shall descend from heaven with a shout, with the voice of the archangel, and with the trump of God: and the dead in Christ shall rise first: then we which are alive and remain shall be caught up together with them in the clouds, to meet the Lord in the air: and so shall we ever be with the Lord*

*Wherefore comfort one another with these words* (I Thes. 4:13 - 18).

## To live for all eternity:

Living for all eternity is a reality with which man must grapple. One must realize that the soul of man is immortal – that it goes on living after the body is dead. What is crucial is where that soul will spend that continuous life. Again we refer to the story of the rich man and Lazarus to see that the rich man maintained consciousness even after he had died. His faculties were intact. He felt pain – he was in torment. He thirsted – he wanted some water from Lazarus. He saw Lazarus in Abraham's bosom. He heard Abraham's response that his requests were denied. He was called upon to remember. Maybe then his mental faculties functioned better than before. He remembered his brothers. He knew that it was possible for them to get to that place of torment. His desire was that they not get to that place. He was asked to remember the good time that he had enjoyed on the earth which he did with regret. These had distracted him from what was really important. Now he had missed out. He was in hell.

Eternal life was not a new concept to man at the time of Christ. Of course we know that Abraham looked for that city whose builder and maker is God. The Pharisees knew about eternal life. Jesus Christ derided the Pharisees for their assumed knowledge when he said to them: *"Search the scriptures; for in them ye think ye have eternal life: and they are they which testify of me"* (Jn. 5:39). They thought they knew the Scriptures yet they knew nothing about Jesus Christ. The message of the Old Testament was about Jesus Christ and they did not know it.

On two different occasions Luke records that persons came to Jesus with that all important question. In Luke 10:25 a Lawyer sought to tempt Jesus with the question. He asked: "Master, what shall I do to inherit eternal life?" Later in His ministry a certain ruler approached Jesus with the question: "Good Master, what shall I do to inherit eternal life?" (Lk. 18:18). They were both well aware that there was life after death and that it was for eternity.

Some other religions also teach life after death. For some it is called reincarnation, where one comes back to this life in another form or as a different person. This is a perversion of the truth but they are aware of a life hereafter. For others it is a utopia where all is bliss. For some it is a time and place for enjoying fair maidens. The fact remains that regardless of the perversion, man is aware of the possibility of life after death.

But God assures us that there is life after death and for the believer in Him it is a life of bliss. For the Christian it is the result of faith. One believes in Christ and it is counted to him for righteousness. The righteousness which man had lost and which he longs for so much is available through faith in Christ.

*My sheep hear my voice, and I know them, and they follow me: and I give unto them eternal life; and they shall never perish, neither shall any man pluck them out of my hand* (Jn. 10:27).

*And this is the will of him that sent me, that every one which seeth the Son, and believeth on him, may have <u>everlasting life</u>: and I will raise him up at the last day* (Jn. 6:40).

*That whosoever <u>believeth</u> in him should not perish, but have <u>eternal life</u>. For God so loved the world, that he gave his only begotten Son, that whosoever believeth in him should not perish, but have <u>everlasting life</u>* (Jn. 3:15, 16).

*He that <u>believeth</u> on the Son hath <u>everlasting life</u>: and he that believeth not the Son shall not see life; but the wrath of God abideth on him* (Jn. 3:36).

*Verily, verily, I say unto you, He that heareth my word, and believeth on him that sent me, hath <u>everlasting life</u>, and shall not come into condemnation; but is <u>passed from death unto life</u>* (Jn. 5:24).

*But now being made free from sin, and become servants to God, ye have your fruit unto holiness, and the end <u>everlasting life</u>* (Rom. 6:22). (Underline mine)

While man seeks a life of bliss, for many it is a life of instant gratification. They live for the here and now. As one colloquialism puts it, "One cannot leave what one has seen now for what one has not yet seen." The Bible says of the woman who lives in pleasure that she is dead while she lives (I Tim. 5:6). The Bible gives us a different take on our life here. Jesus said to His disciples: *"These things I have spoken unto you, that in me ye might have peace. In the world ye shall have tribulation: but be of good cheer; I have overcome the world"* (Jn. 16:33).

## The restoration of all things:

Since the fall in the Garden of Eden, all of creation is under the curse of sin. Because of sin there is not the ease of life as there might have been. The earth ceased to produce like it did, pain and suffering and hard work became man's lot. The day is coming when these things will be reversed. Creation, like man, awaits man's restoration because it, too, will be restored. Paul states it this way:

> *For I reckon that the sufferings of this present time are not worthy to be compared with the glory which shall be revealed in us.*
>
> *For the earnest expectation of the creature* (plant and animal kingdoms*) waiteth for the manifestation of the sons of God (*mankind*). For the creature was made subject to vanity, not willingly, but by reason of him who hath subjected the same in hope, because the creature itself also shall be delivered from the bondage of corruption into the glorious liberty of the children of God.*
>
> *For we know that the whole creation groaneth and travaileth in pain together until now. And not only they, but ourselves also, which have the firstfruits of the Spirit, even we ourselves groan within ourselves, waiting for the adoption, to wit, the redemption of our body.*
>
> *For we are saved by hope: but hope that is seen is not hope: for what a man seeth, why doth he yet hope for? But if we hope for that we see not, then do we with patience wait for it* (Rom. 8:18 – 25).

The hope of all things is restoration. Man is said to have died because he had life. When Adam sinned, man became subject to death. Christ came to restore that life back to man and he, with great anticipation, waits for it. But God does not operate in our framework. Man operates in the now. For him time is not guaranteed. God, on the other hand is not affected by time and days or years are within His 'soon'. There is order, too, in what He does. Restoration will take place but in a particular order.

> *For as in Adam all die, even so in Christ shall all be made alive. But every man in his own order: Christ the first-fruits; afterward they that are Christ's at his coming. Then cometh the end, when he shall have delivered up the kingdom to God, even the Father; when he shall have put down all rule and all authority and power. For he must reign, till he hath put all enemies under his feet. The last enemy that shall be destroyed is death* (I Cor. 15:22 – 26).

Even the process of restoration holds its enigma. Paul seeks to unravel the puzzle through the inspiration afforded him by Christ. Several poignant questions are addressed which, as Paul anticipates, will be posited by those brave enough to ask.

> *But some man will say, How are the dead raised up? And with what body do they come?*
> *Thou fool, that which thou sowest is not quickened, except it die: And that which thou sowest, thou sowest not that body that shall be, but bare grain, it may chance of wheat, or of some other grain: but God giveth it a body as it hath pleased him, and to every seed his own body.*

*All flesh is not the same flesh: but there is one kind of flesh of men, another flesh of beasts, another of fishes, and another of birds. There are also celestial bodies, and bodies terrestrial: but the glory of the celestial is one, and the glory of the terrestrial is another.*

*There is one glory of the sun, and another glory of the moon, and another glory of the stars: for one star differeth from another star in glory. So also is the resurrection of the dead. It is sown in corruption; it is raised in incorruption: it is sown in dishonour; it is raised in glory: it is sown in weakness; it is raised in power; it is sown a natural body; it is raised a spiritual body. There is a natural body, and there is a spiritual body* (I Cor. 15:35 – 44).

## The reward of the believer:

The Christian anticipates a restoration of all that He had lost. But God promises more than just what was lost. There is much to gain for a life lived for God. For enduring temptation and tribulation there is a crown of life. For faithful service to God, man has the expectation of ruling and reigning with Christ for a thousand years. To those who are thirsty drink from the fountain of the water of life. One cannot help but think of the rich man in hell at this time. To those who overcome they will inherit all things. To all is available the tree of life. One can bask in the presence of God in a new heaven and a new earth where the Son is the light and there is no night there.

*Blessed is the man that endureth temptation: for when he is tried, he shall receive the crown of life, which the Lord hath promised to them that love him* (Ja. 1:12).

*Fear none of those things which thou shalt suffer:
behold, the devil shall cast some of you into prison,
that ye may be tried; and ye shall have tribulation
ten days: be thou faithful unto death, and I will give
thee a crown of life.* (Rev. 2:10)

*And I saw thrones, and they sat upon them, and
judgment was given unto them: and I saw the souls of
them that were beheaded for the witness of Jesus, and
for the word of God, and which had not worshipped
the beast, neither his image, neither had received his
mark upon their foreheads, or in their hands; and
they lived and reigned with Christ a thousand years.*

*But the rest of the dead lived not again until
the thousand years were finished. This is the first
resurrection.*

*Blessed and holy is he that hath part in the first
resurrection: on such the second death hath no power,
but they shall be priests of God and of Christ, and shall
reign with him a thousand years* (Rev. 20:4 – 6).

*And he said unto me, It is done. I am Alpha and
Omega, the beginning and the end. I will give unto
him that is athirst of the fountain of the water of life
freely. He that overcometh shall inherit all things; and I
will be his God, and he shall be my son* (Rev. 21:6, 7).

*And he showed me a pure river of water of life, clear
as crystal, proceeding out of the throne of God and of
the Lamb.*

*In the midst of the street of it, and on either side
of the river, was there the tree of life, which bare
twelve manner of fruits, and yielded her fruit every
month: and the leaves of the tree were for the healing
of the nations. And there shall be no more curse: but*

*the throne of God and of the Lamb shall be in it; and his servants shall serve him:*

*And they shall see his face; and his name shall be in their foreheads. And there shall be no night there; and they need no candle, neither light of the sun; for the Lord God giveth them light: and they shall reign for ever and ever.*

*And he said unto me, 'These sayings are faithful and true: and the Lord God of the holy prophets sent his angel to show unto his servants the things which must shortly be done'* (Rev. 22:1 – 6).

The believer in Christ has much to look forward to. It is a shame for anyone who would read the Scriptures and least of all the words of this book to miss out on the blessed promises of God. One would be the product of one's own pride and arrogance to reject the grand provision of God in favor of one's own conception.

*Be not deceived; God is not mocked: for whatsoever a man soweth, that shall he also reap. For he that soweth to his flesh shall of the flesh reap corruption; but he that soweth to the Spirit shall of the Spirit reap life everlasting* (Gal. 6:7, 8).

# END NOTES

1. Arnold, Bill T.; *Encountering the Book of Genesis*; Baker Books, 1998, p. 46, 47
2. Anderson, Sir Norman; *The World's Religions*; William B. Erdman's Publishing Co.; Grand Rapids, Michigan; 1975, p. 13, 14
3. http://en.wikipedia.org/wiki/*Religion*
4. http://en.wikipedia.org/wiki/*Religion*
5. Wikipedia; the free encyclopedia, *deity*
6. Wikipedia; the free encyclopedia, *deity*
7. Wikipedia; the free encyclopedia, *scriptures*
8. Wikipedia; the free encyclopedia, *morality*
9. Wikipedia, the free encyclopedia, *morality*
10. http://wikipedia.org/wiki/*lifestance*
11. http://wikipedia.org/wiki/*lifestance*
12. http://wikipedia.org/wiki/lifestance
13. http://wikipedia.org/wiki/lifestance
14. Wikipedia; the free encyclopedia,
15. Geisler, Norman L.; Christian Apologetics, prince Press 1976; p. 69
16. Geisler, Christian Apologetics, 1976; p. 69
17. Geisler, Christian Apologetics, 1976; p. 69
18. Geisler, Christian Apologetics, 1976; p. 69
19. Geisler, Christian Apologetics, 1976; p. 72
20. Geisler, Christian Apologetics, 1976; p. 49

21. Urah, Bob; © 2009 WorldNetDaily, posted January 16th 2009
22. Urah, Bob; January 16th 2009
23. Urah, Bob; January 16th 2009
24. Urah, Bob; January 16th 2009
25. Urah, Bob; January 16th 2009
26. Urah, Bob; January 16th 2009
27. Urah, Bob; January 16th 2009
28. Urah, Bob; January 16th 2009
29. Geisler, Christian Apologetics, 1976; p. 53
30. Geisler, Christian Apologetics, 1976; p. 53
31. www.answers.com
32. www.gotquestions.org/cult-definitions-christian.html
33. www.gotquestions.org/denominations-christian.html
34. Martin, Walter, The Kingdom of the Cults, pg.11
35. Martin, Walter, The Kingdom of the Cults, pg.17
36. www.answers.com/topic/denomination
37. dictionary.reference.com/browse/cult
38. www.cultdefinition.com
39. www.cultdefinition.com
40. www.cultdefinition.com
41. www.gotquestions.org/cult-definitions.html
42. www.religioustolerance.org/cults.html
43. www.wikipedia.org/wiki/sect
44. www.wikipedia.org/wiki/sect
45. www.religioustolerance.org/cults.html
46. Young, Robert, Analytical Concordance of the Bible; p. 477
47. Thayer's Greek-English Lexicon, p. 16
48. Geisler; Christian Apologetics; p. 343, 344
49. Geisler; Christian Apologetics; p. 344
50. Geisler; Christian Apologetics; p. 344
51. http://en.wikipedia.org/wiki/article (grammar)
52. http://en.wikipedia.org/wiki/truth
53. Geisler; Christian Apologetics, p. 94
54. Dictionary.com

# BIBLIOGRAPHY

Anderson, Sir Norman, *The World's Religions*, Grand Rapids; William B. Eerdmans Publishing Company; 1975

Arnold, Bill T.; *Encountering The Book Of Genesis*; Baker Books; 1998,

Geisler, Norman L. *Christian Apologetics*, Grand Rapids; Prince Press; 1976

Martin, Walter, *The Kingdom of the Cults*, Minneapolis, Bethany House Publishers, 1965

Thayer, Joseph Henry D.D., *Thayer's Greek-English Lexicon Of The New Testament*, Grand Rapids, Associated Publishers and Authors Inc.,

Young, Robert, *Analytical Concordance of the Bible*, Hendrickson Publishers

Unra, Bob; © 2009 WorldNet Daily, posted January 16th 2009

http://en.wikipedia.org/wiki/Religion

Wikipedia, The Free Encyclopedia, *Deity*

Wikipedia, The Free Encyclopedia, *Scriptures*

Wikipedia, The Free Encyclopedia, *Morality*

Wikipedia, The Free Encyclopedia, *Life stance*

www.answers.com

www.answers.com/topic/denomination

www.Dictionary.reference.com/brouse/cult

www.cultdefinition.com

www.gotquestions.org/**cult-definition**.html

*www.gotquestions.org/***denominations***-Christian.html*

www.religioustolerance.org/cults.html

www.wikipedia.org/wiki/**Sect**

http://en.wikipedia.org/wiki/Article_(grammar)

http://en.wikipedia.org/wiki/Truth

www.ingramcontent.com/pod-product-compliance
Lightning Source LLC
Chambersburg PA
CBHW021622120626
46545CB00001B/355